T0193191

SAINT PIO'S BLESSING

Jane Donnelly DIP/Psych

BALBOA.
PRESS
A DIVISION OF HAY HOUSE

Balboa Press books may be ordered through booksellers or by contacting:

Balboa Press
A Division of Hay House
1663 Liberty Drive
Bloomington, IN 47403
www.balboapress.com
1 (877) 407-4847

Because of the dynamic nature of the Internet, any web addresses or links contained in this book may have changed since publication and may no longer be valid. The views expressed in this work are solely those of the author and do not necessarily reflect the views of the publisher, and the publisher hereby disclaims any responsibility for them.

The author of this book does not dispense medical advice or prescribe the use of any technique as a form of treatment for physical, emotional, or medical problems without the advice of a physician, either directly or indirectly. The intent of the author is only to offer information of a general nature to help you in your quest for emotional and spiritual well-being. In the event you use any of the information in this book for yourself, which is your constitutional right, the author and the publisher assume no responsibility for your actions.

Any people depicted in stock imagery provided by Thinkstock are models, and such images are being used for illustrative purposes only.
Certain stock imagery © Thinkstock.

Disclaimer
All clients mentioned in this book are fictional and are a compression of cases used to tell the story. No such events actually took place.

Print information available on the last page.

ISBN: 978-1-5043-7701-0 (sc)
ISBN: 978-1-5043-7703-4 (hc)
ISBN: 978-1-5043-7702-7 (e)

Library of Congress Control Number: 2017904190

Balboa Press rev. date: 06/09/2017

CONTENTS

Dedication vii

Acknowledgment xi

Introduction xiii

Chapter 1   The Beginning 1

Chapter 2   Moving Forward 7

Chapter 3   Guided Adventures 22

Chapter 4   The Healing House (An Teach) 34

Chapter 5   Testing Times 46

Chapter 6   Being a Medium 61

Chapter 7   Carrying On 80

Chapter 8   Saint Pio 89

Afterword 111

Biography 117

DEDICATION

I dedicate this book to Saint Pio of Pietrelcina

And to my hugely supportive husband Mike

With infinite love and gratitude.

"Pray, pray to the Lord with me, because the whole world needs prayer.

And every day when your heart especially feels the loneliness of life, pray.

Pray to the Lord, because even God needs our prayers."

Padre Pio of Pietrelcina

ACKNOWLEDGMENT

Ghlóir le Dia sna Harda

Glory to God in the Highest

INTRODUCTION

Monday the 4th of July 2016 started out as just an ordinary day. The date is not a special one for most of us here in Ireland but we do think of all our family and friends in the U.S.A celebrating independence on that day. I am a self employed healer, spirit medium, Angel therapist, Reiki Master and shop owner. That day I had some clients for healings and it was a lovely sunny day. I was able to enjoy some sunshine between clients so I was thoroughly enjoying working from home and feeling so grateful that I was not stuck indoors on a day like that one. My client list was building steadily and I love what I do. That night I went to bed at 10.30pm and fell asleep almost instantly. In the early hours of the morning I awoke to a feeling that there was a presence in the room with me, my husband was at work so I wondered who it could be. To my utter amazement I saw Saint Pio standing there and he gave me a blessing! But I am getting way ahead of myself here, so I better begin this story where I now know it all began! The series of incidents and synchronicities which have led me to this moment, as I now write of my life, and experiences with Saint Pio of Pietrelcina for you are in fact quiet remarkable.

CHAPTER 1

The Beginning

This story begins on the 10th of March 2014 that was the day I became self employed, in my own little Angel shop in Killarney, County Kerry. God and the angels had guided me to this special moment, where I was going to bring the angels to Kerry in a new way! My task as I understood it was, to bring God and the angels into people's everyday awareness so they could feel the loving guidance that I am blessed to feel every day.

I had previously been a retail manager in a large fast paced retail outlet so it came as a shock to me, to be working in my own relaxed little shop with no employees and no co workers. I quickly realized that a lesson I really needed to learn was patience! I had purchased a deck of Angel Cards the previous year and through the cards I was guided to leave my job and set up on my own, selling angel books and other spiritual items. My shop was open about two weeks when I became a Certified Angel Card Reader, I completed a course with Doreen Virtue, and Doreen is the beautiful lady who created the Angel Cards that I now owned. It was an awesome course and I learnt so much and my faith grew so much too. I love reading the cards for people and watching their surprise, and amazement as the angel messages are always correct. I also love reading the cards for myself and the clarity and guidance I receive which is awesome and invaluable!

A few months later I was guided to become a Reiki Master and then I knew something, It dawned on me that I have always been a healer, I was just somewhat unaware if it! Years earlier I had held one ladies arthritic hands just to warm them and after about five minutes they opened up and never again gave her any trouble! My children and I hardly ever went to a doctor; I always treated them with my hands or used natural remedies. My life had suddenly become so stress free and happy, ever since the angels had entered it. I began to say thank you Angels so often! I was settling in nicely by the time summer ended and I had my first summer as my own boss under my belt. I still wasn't making a proper wage but with my husband's huge support to me, we were getting by alright.

I was on my own one morning in September when a lady walked into the shop and came straight to the counter. She then placed a bottle of water in front of me and said "Hello, Lionel said to give you this, It's from Saint Michaels healing well ".I said are you sure it's for me, as I don't know anything about it?" She then said "Are you Jane?" and I smiled and said "I am ". She smiled back at me and said "Well this water is definitely for you because that is what he said!" she then turned around and walked out the door! I was absolutely gob smacked, who was this lady, and more importantly who was Lionel? What healing well was she talking about and where was it? Boy was I puzzled! I plugged in the computer and powered it on, I had to try find out something before I cracked myself up! When it was ready, I opened the browser and searched for Saint Michaels well. A link came up with a caption "Hundreds flock to Holy Shrine" I was intrigued so I clicked on it.

I read about this sacred site named after Saint Michael the Archangel. My heart almost skipped a beat, I love the

Archangel Michael and pray and talk to him daily. I could not believe this Holy space was so near to me, within the county borders. This was amazing; just wait until I tell Mike I thought! I continued reading; the well is built on a site where there once was an ancient well.

This well was built in 1958 and it features a statue of Saint Michael defeating Satan. It is a centre for healing and prayer. I was excited beyond words! I just could not believe how blessed we are to have this hidden gem on our doorstep! I then searched for images of the well; I could hardly wait to see what it looked like. I opened the images and oh my, oh my, it was spectacular! I felt that I was strongly guided to go this place and I was feeling very excited. Later in the day Mike came in to see me and I made him a cup of tea and told him all about the lady with the healing water and Saint Michaels well. I opened up images on the computer and showed Mike the well, he was amazed, and it was so beautiful! We talked excitedly about going there and we decided we would set off the next free Sunday we had on a trip to the well. With that decided I returned to work and back to reality.

It was Sunday 5th October 2014 when we headed off to Saint Michael the Archangels healing well. It was dull, cloudy and a very cold wintery day so we wrapped up warm for our day out. All four of us went, Mike, I and the two youngest children, Hannah (aged 5) and Michael (aged 3 and a half!). It was not a long drive and in about half an hour we arrived at our destination. Mike parked the car at the side of the road; we could see the top of the well from there. We saw a sign and walked to it and then we saw a gate leading down to the well. Mike opened the gate and we all went through and he closed it again after us. We made our way down the winding path and it was lined with colorful plants and flowers. It was very beautiful, when we got to the end of the path we entered the well area and it was a sight to be seen! I had never seen a life size statue of Saint Michael the Archangel, it was so big and so life like! The energy there was very powerful, it was awesome! All of a sudden the sun came out and the grey sky disappeared, we had to take off our hats and gloves as we were getting too warm! I took a moment and closed my eyes, I felt so blessed to be standing right here. There are seven prayer points around the well and each numbered spot has healing properties to different body parts. I began at number one and prayed my way round the well. I then went and sat on a chair at the top of the well, I closed my eyes and the sun felt so warm on my face. It was Heavenly! I could sense and feel the angels surrounding me and I was filled with such an intense feeling of peace. After a while I stood up and told Mike he should have a go, on the seat with his eyes closed. I walked around the seating area and read the prayers stuck onto the walls, it really was a special place. There was a stack of water bottles so we filled two to take home for those we knew who were sick. We had read that the water had healing properties and when to drink it and how much needed to receive healing from it. It was over an hour later when we left the well.

It was January 2015 when we next returned to Saint Michael's well. We encountered the same peaceful powerful energy, the same as the first day we came here. This was such a beautiful, sacred, healing space. Just like the first time the sun came out and the sky turned blue! Was Archangel Michael doing this for us I thought? Thank you Saint Michael if you are I said as I smiled to myself.

My first Christmas in the shop had been very busy and I was up to my eyes in gift baskets! I was so thankful for the angels guiding me to this new life. The unit next door to my shop was available for rent and it was much larger than the one i was in. My shop was full to bursting with a lot of new stock lines and expansion of other lines. In the second week of January 2015 I asked Mike to go speak with the landlord about moving Donnelly's into a bigger retail unit in the Shopping Arcade. Things were really starting to move now! In a few weeks the unit next door would be ready for us to move into. I was actively meditating for quiet some time now and I really loved the experience and the changes it was bringing to my awareness. I sat in this sacred space and meditated for some time and the peace and calm that came over me was out of this world!

One night later in the month, Mike and I sat down to do a past life regression meditation .I am fascinated by past life stories and experiences so I was really excited to be trying this for the first time in the comfort of our own home. I had recently purchased a deck of past life regression oracle cards which had really whetted my appetite. It was a revelation to me that we are souls having a human experience not humans with a soul! I found this information resonated with my soul strongly and the universe was finally beginning to make sense to me. We settled down and began listening to the guided meditation that would bring us back to a life we lived in the past. Eek! I was super excited! The meditation was beautiful and it brought me very deep into subconscious levels. Here is what I saw when I entered the door to the past. I saw myself as a lady with deeply sallow skin. I was somewhere in the Mediterranean and the weather was warm and sunny. I could see my little house; it was a one or two room tiny house in the midst of other tiny houses. There were flowers on the windows and steps and it looked a bit run down but lovely at the same time. I was now inside my home and a lady came to me for me to heal her, we were speaking Italian, I did not know this lady before this day, she had come from a nearby town to receive healing from me as I was the lady who healed with my hands. I was then instructed in the meditation to go to the end of this life and see what happened. I saw my body being carried out of my home in a coffin. The coffin was being carried by six men who were dressed respectfully, but their clothes had a working class look on them. I sensed we were poor but happy people. I knew I had lived to a great old age and I was happy to go. I was up above looking down on this narrow laneway as they carried the coffin with my physical body inside. This image was so real and so vivid, I could see the tiny houses, the flowers and I could even smell the roses! Soon it was time for me to return to the room I was sitting in and the meditation was over. I was truly amazed by the amount of detail I had received and with such clarity. Mike and I shared our experiences and Mike was over awed when I told him about my journey into the past! I had absolutely no idea what it all meant but it resonated deep within me that this was a small part of a larger picture. I would just have to have patience until it fitted in!

CHAPTER 2

Moving Forward

The third week of February arrived and it was then we got the keys to the new unit and were able to begin setting it up for the new bigger and brighter Donnelly's shop. It was a beautiful bright unit and the energy in there was amazing. On the 20th of February we were taking stock from the back area and moving it. It was not too far to trek with it, but there was so much stuff to go! Michael (now age 4) and I were clearing out a cubby hole, near the table were the children used to sit, eat and play. I was walking towards the shop from the back and Michael was following behind me when he said "Mom there is a lady sitting in the wall." I turned around and looked at the wall and I could not see her but I did not doubt Michael could see her, so I asked him is she nice"? He replied" yes, she is smiling." I said "what else is she doing?" Michael replied "she is making a hat ". I then said "well say goodbye to her, as we must keep moving these things". The next few hours we were all busy sorting stock in the new unit and I totally forgot about our conversation. The minute I got home that night which was about 11 pm I could not get that lady out of my mind. Over the past few years Mike and I had been researching our family trees so I knew where to look to find information on this lady. I just had to find out why she was there and who she was, what was her name? I the remembered when I first opened the shop the picture frames used to be on the floor in the morning and never broken after a big fall off a shelf onto a wooden floor. I did begin to think the place was haunted but quickly told myself not to be silly, there had to be a rational explanation, now thinking back it seems that lady in spirit was trying to get my attention. The locks on the shutter doors used to change direction in the early days too! It opened clockwise one day and anticlockwise another! I powered on the computer once the children were in bed and I went in search of the lady in the wall. I went in to the census records and after a little detective work and figuring out the old number system to relate to the current address I found her! My heart skipped a beat as I opened the record, I knew it in my bones this was her. I had no idea how I knew it but I was confident this was in fact her. I read through the details and I then turned to Mike and said "What is a milliner?" and he replied "someone who makes hats ".I could not breathe, oh my God I found her I shrieked! I read the details aloud to Mike and he agreed that this could very possibly be the lady in the wall. I was certain this was her, so I got my alter cloth out and some candles and an angel and I prayed for that lady's soul to go to heaven and reunite with her family. I felt such peace in my heart that after a little while I knew she had gone to the light and was in Heaven and I blew out the candles and went to bed totally exhausted but happy.

It was an arduous job packing up the entire shop lock, stock and shelving units but with a few very late nights and the help of God and the angels we were ready to open on Saturday 21st February 2015 which was the next day. I went in to work early to get things in order and I opened the doors at 9am.The shop looked amazing, I absolutely loved it! I pottered around arranging the angels in a beautiful display; it was wonderful to have the space to display everything properly. I took a break at 10.30am, while I was standing behind the counter near the cash register when I noticed somebody standing to the right of me on the outside of the counter. I turned my head to look at who was there and I saw a gentleman dressed in the attire of someone from the early 1900's! He was wearing a dark suit and a high top hat; he had a big moustache and a tidy beard. He was leaning against the counter with one arm and as I looked at him he smiled and tipped his hat towards me .I blinked and he was gone! He was the lady from the wall's husband! Oh my God, he had come to say thank you to me. My heart was fit to burst when I thought of them reunited after all those years and for her that she was now where she needed to be. Life is amazing and can be so magical! I took a moment to thank God for giving me the ability to send souls to the light, I was not sure of exactly what I was saying but it felt right to say it just then.

The next few weeks were all go, with putting the finishing touches and paint jobs in the back rooms of the new shop. On Sunday 12th April we set off to Saint Michaels well again. Mikes dad had not been so well recently so we wanted to get some healing water for him and I wanted some for my mother too. As Mike was driving along, we were about halfway there when I turned to look at him and said "can we go to the church there as well today? It is also called after Michael the Archangel". As I said those words an image came to my mind of a beautiful church with a round stained glass circle in the front of it. Mike replied and said" we can go there but how do know about the church? I replied "I have no idea how I know that" and I described the image I had just seen. Mike then said" which one will we go to first the well or the church?" I replied "we should go to the well first as it is on the way to the church and the church is further into the village on the right hand side ". (I had never been to that village or church before, I had no idea how I knew any of this). Mike continued driving and I sat quietly thinking would the church I saw in my minds eye be the actual church and would it be where I said it was? That would be absolutely mad if it was I thought! We stopped on the road outside the well and made our way through the gate and walked to the well. Just as before the sun came out and the sky turned blue, was it always sunny here I thought! It turned out to be a beautiful day and I took some photographs to show my friends of this wonderful place I had been telling them about. Some beautiful orbs showed up in these pictures and I was not surprised because the energy there on that day was different and more powerful, I could feel it. We stayed for about an hour and then we all piled in to the car to go find the church.

Mike drove towards the village and as he turned the corner we could see the steeple of the church and it appeared to be on the left side of the road from here. Mikes said "on the right you said wasn't it?" I replied "yes that is what I was shown ". Low and behold as we approached Saint Michael's church it was in fact on the right hand side of the road! Oh my God it was exactly as I had seen it! What did this all mean? I was excited about it but I had no idea what was going on! We all walked in to the church and it was very beautiful. We knelt and said some prayers before walking around to look at the statues and light some candles. As we walked back down the church I noticed a room off to the right, so we made our way over to it and went inside. There were these two huge glass doors leading into the room. There was a life size statue of Padre Pio standing on a water feature of flowing water, with a kneeler in front of it. Either side of the statue there was prayers written on the wall.

In front of the most beautiful stained glass window were four chairs facing the statue and off to the side there was a first class relic of Padre Pio's in a glass case with a stand of candles that could be lit for intentions. It was beautiful! The energy in this sacred space was incredible!

I kneeled and prayed in front of Padre Pio's statue and instantly the feeling of peace and calmness in the entire room magnified. I'm not sure how long I stayed like this, I could have stayed there forever I felt, but I was not alone so I got up and let Mike have his turn there. As Mike was praying I walked outside the room to give him some privacy and to enjoy the energy alone in there. It really is such a wonderful room. Just outside the door was a big book on Padre Pio's life. I skimmed through the pages and it opened at a page where Padre Pio had lived as a child. My heart almost stopped…that was the very same place I had seen in my past life regression meditation months ago! What did this mean? How was this possible, I was not making sense of much of these happenings lately? When Mike came out of the room I showed him the book and then I opened the page to where Pio lived as a child and I reminded Mike of that past life experience I had in Italy, he remembered the details. I then pointed to the page and I could hardly speak as I said "that was the place in my meditation". Mike said "where was that?" and I had to search the book for a reference to Pietrelcina.The place name meant nothing to me, as far as I knew anyway! Had I known Padre Pio in a past life, is that what this meant?" This was such an amazing experience and I was feeling somewhat overwhelmed. We lit some candles and said some prayers before we set off on our journey home. All that evening I could not get Padre Pio out of my head. So after the children were tucked up in bed I went on the computer to look up Padre Pio and get some information. I really knew very little about him. This is what I read that" Padre Pio was born Francesco Forgione to Gieuseppa and Grazio in the small farming town of Pietrelcina in 1887. As a young boy, Francesco showed extraordinary gifts of grace and at the age of five he dedicated his life to God. His mother described him as a quiet boy who showed a love for the religious life of spirit. As a young boy he could communicate with Jesus, Mary and his Guardian Angel. At twenty three he was ordained into the priesthood. He prayed almost continuously, he loved to pray the rosary. He suffered ill health form the age of nine and after his ordination he had to remain at home due to ill health. For more than five years he was separated form his religious community. The stigmata or the wounds of Christ appeared on him in September 1918 while he was praying before a crucifix. He was thirty one years old and the first stigmatized priest in history. He bore these painful wounds on his hands, feet and side for over fifty years. In addition God also endowed Padre Pio with many extraordinary gifts including healing, bio location, prophesy, miracles, the gift of tongues, the gift of conversion and the ability to read hearts, the grace to see angelic beings and the fragrance which emanated from his wounds which frequently announced his invisible presence. He always remained humble constantly at the disposal of almighty God. Padre Pio passed away at the age of eighty one on September 23rd 1968. He had often declared "after my death I will do more. My real mission will begin after my death ".In one of the largest liturgies in the Vatican's history Pope John Paul II canonized Padre Pio in 2002 on June 16th .The Pope said " Prayer and charity – this is the most concrete synthesis of Padre Pio's teachings". Saint Pio's life might be summed up in the words of Saint Paul to the Colossians " Now I rejoice in my sufferings for your sake, and in my flesh I complete what is lacking in Christ's afflictions for the sake of his body, that is the church ".Saint Pio's body was placed in a crypt at Saint Mary of Graces in 1968.The body was later exhumed in 2008 and displayed for veneration of the faithful until 2009.In 2010 the body was transferred in the new San Pio church and placed to rest in the golden crypt". Saint Pio of Pietrelcina pray for us."

I was amazed and astounded at what I had read about Saint Pio, what a remarkable soul he was! And I felt all the richer knowing more about this very special man. I still had no idea what it meant with the past life regression and the church and now the book earlier in the day but I was sure feeling very blessed just by the association to this most honorable man.

The following morning I got up early and sat in meditation for half an hour, it was blissful! After that I got ready to go open the shop and I was in early and opened up at ten to nine. I had been reading the New Testament in the bible on and off for some months now and today I decided I would finish reading it! During the week I was out in the garden one evening and I was taking some photographs. I was taking pictures of the birds at the bird feeder and when I looked through my camera I could see rainbow orbs flying around the birds. Wow, wow, wow they were awesome! I had only recently begun to see orbs and marveled at such beauty and their ability to communicate with us! I do so love the angels. I was now rising earlier each morning to go outside and watch the sunrise and do my gratitude and prayers out there. Those mornings were magical. Everyone should take the time to just sit and watch the sunrise and the sunset everyday that they can.

On Thursday 16th April I woke up at 6.30am and got myself out of bed to sit for meditation and prayer time. As I was meditating I heard these words "you alone are the Holy one, you alone are most high. You alone are the most High Jesus Christ. Believe these words for they are your truth, your light and your way. For he who believes in me shall never die. Keep to the path and you shall find you way home". Was that Jesus I just heard, or God I had no idea! That was totally amazing! I immediately got my diary and wrote it down before I could forget it! I was thrilled to have received this divine guidance and so very grateful for this spiritual connection. That day was amazing in every way; it was as if angels were walking beside me making everything work out perfectly!

The next morning I started my day outside with the sunrise again. It was a beautiful morning; it is so easy to be grateful on mornings like these, when I feel the blessings of the world around me. I had a lovely deep meditation once I came inside and afterwards I had a very strong urge to pray to Jesus. When I tried to think of a prayer I realized I didn't know any prayers to Jesus. Had I ever known one, I couldn't remember? I had a busy day in the shop with readings and healings as well as shop work. When I sat for my lunch, that urge to pray to Jesus returned so I searched for Jesus prayer on the shop computer.

Prayer to Jesus

"Sacred heart of Jesus today I wish to live in you, in your Grace in which I desire at all costs to persevere. Keep me from sin and strengthen my will by helping me to keep watch over my senses, my imagination and my heart. Help me to correct my faults which are the source of sin. I beg you to do this, Oh Jesus through Mary, Your immaculate mother

"Lord Jesus Christ, Son Of God have mercy on me "Amen.

"Jesus our Lord and Brother, save us in your love "Amen.

These are such beautiful prayers, I began to say these daily added to my other prayers and I really felt the closeness to Jesus that my soul needed. The next day was Saturday and I was working the shop, no clients just shop work so a relaxed and easy day in some ways. I opened up the shop and lit an incense to set the tone for the day, peace and love! I did a quick walk of the shop to ensure it was tidy and everything was ready for the day. I went to play a cd and as I was about to press play when an idea came to me to listen to the radio instead. I switched sources and the radio came on. There was a programme on the radio about the bog slide in Kerry that happened in 1896, it was called the moving bog.

As I briefly mentioned earlier Mike and I had been researching our family tree genealogy for years. Some time last year we were able to trace Mike's family to the family in this story and they were related when we went back through the generations. It was on the night of Sunday 28th December 1896 in Gneeveguilla, after a long period of bad weather that the people of the area were woken in the night by the sound of something like and earthquake. In the morning they quickly realized to their shock and amazement that 200 acres of bog land was on the move towards Killarney town taking everything in its way with it.

The moving bog claimed the lives of all but one family member and their livestock. The family involved in this tragedy was Donnelly's. Con and Johanna Donnelly and five of their children died that night. They had six children in all; Daniel, Hannah, Humphrey, Katie, Margaret and Lizzie. Katie was the only family member who survived as she had spent the night in her grandmother's house. My heart went out to these poor people who had perished in this way and I silently prayed for their souls.

I felt heartbroken after listening to the show and hearing the local stories that had carried down the generations since then of that fateful night for the Donnelly family. I wasn't sure was it the family connection to my husband and children that had me feeling this way. Or was there some other reason? Either way I was feeling delicate and sad. Luckily the shop was busy with customers so it took my mind of things. At 2 o clock Mike and the children called in to have lunch with me. It did not take long until I began to tell Mike about the radio show I had listened to earlier. Mike told me that that area was only a few miles from town to where that all had happened. He said there is a plaque on the side of the road in remembrance of the Donnelly's of Gneeveguilla. We talked a little more on those poor people and we then decided that tomorrow being Sunday we would take the short drive up there and pay our respects. I felt a lot better knowing we would go there tomorrow but I did not know why I was feeling better because of that! I wasn't making sense even to myself.

The next morning I woke up at 7 am, I felt the need to do some deep grounding. I went outside barefoot and walked on the grass. I had brought a blanket with me to sit on and I placed it under a tree. I sat to meditate in nature and absorbed all that beautiful healing grounding energy. I sat there for twenty minutes and felt rejuvenated and energized afterwards. Oh what a beautiful day it was! I went inside to catch up on some housework before Mike and the children got up. After a late breakfast we all got ourselves ready to go for the drive.

We collected Mike's dad and his sister as they too wanted to come with us. Mike was driving and he knew the general area to drive to and found the area without much problem. Mike parked the car at the side of the road and we all got out and walked across the road to the site of the moving bog. When we got to the plaque we stopped and read of the tragic events that happened here to the Donnelly family. Oh my, it really was so shocking and so sad! I took out my phone and took some pictures of Mike and his dad standing either side of the plaque. I also took some of the general area and of Mike's sister too. I could feel the presence of spirit so strongly around us all, as I took the pictures. All of a sudden I felt very unwell. My head felt very heavy and I felt ill. I said to Mike "I'm just going to sit in the car". I did not want to alarm him by telling him how bad I felt, so I went and sat in the car in the hopes of feeling better if I rested. As I settled into my seat in the car I began to feel worse! My head began to pound and the pressure in my forehead felt like it would explode. I had the most violent headache and my eyes were sensitive to the daylight also. I waited for what seemed like forever for the rest of them to return to the car and I put on my bravest face and said I was feeling ok when asked. Mike started up the car and we began our journey back home. What was wrong with me? I was feeling truly awful. I prayed to God to help me. "Three of those souls need to be sent to the light" is what I heard as we pulled away from the area. Who had said that? The further we got from there the better I began to feel. This was very strange. What was going on? I still had the bad headache when we returned home so I drank a glass of water and sat down for a few minutes. Mike then asked me if I was ok and said that I looked very pale. I told him what happened up there and what I heard when leaving there. I then said "three of those souls involved in that tragic event need to be sent to Heaven". As soon as I said those words out loud, the headache lifted out the top of my head! I still felt nauseous and not fully myself.

I got my alter cloth out and some angels and candles too. I did not remember the names of all the Donnelly's who passed away in 1896 and I did not know which ones needed saving. I went and got my phone and I looked up the story online and I began to write the names of all who had perished that night on a piece of paper and I wrote each name I got a sensation on each name, so by the time I had them all written, I knew which souls needed to be saved. I got out my prayer sheets and lit the candles. I called on Archangel Michael to protect me and help me. I began to pray and then I called out the names one by one and sent each one to the light to reunite them with their family and God. As soon as this was done, the heaviness and sickness left my body. I knew in my heart and soul that they were all happy to be together again in Heaven, over one hundred years later. I could feel it in every fiber of my body. I kneeled and prayed for all their souls and the souls of all those who have departed. I thanked God and The Archangel Michael for the guidance and support I had received, and my ability to do this work for the lost souls. Later that night I remembered my need for the deep grounding earlier in the morning and I laughed. Someone knew I would need that for today before I knew myself and for that I felt extremely thankful.

Meditation has enhanced my intuition and opened me up to receive divine wisdom for that I will be eternally grateful and blessed. I was tired after my eventful day so I went to bed early and drifted off to sleep with a subliminal meditation playing .I had such a deep sleep that night, I had no idea even what day it was when I woke up the next morning!

The next few weeks went by happily, I was continuing to rise early to watch the sunrise and meditate before my day in the real world began. One Thursday night I lit some candles and incense and sat for a meditation in the dining room at home. The energy in the room was very high, so high I could almost hear it! I did an angel meditation which was blissful and I slowly floated back to the room and reality. I could feel the angels with me; the energy was amazing there. I went and got my phone so I could take some pictures. I felt I would be able to capture some of this energy. As I looked through the camera lens I could see a colored orb dancing around the candles on the table. It was so beautiful to watch it dance over and back, and then it was joined by another one! Oh my goodness it was a spectacular sight to see. So fantastic! I took some photographs and then I just sat and enjoyed the moment. I felt so blessed. Thank you God, and thank you angels.

I was doing an online course to develop my intuitive and spiritual abilities and part of my course work was to connect and communicate with spirit. This had been happening to me all of my life as far back as I could remember, so I felt I better try understanding it and developing these gifts God has given me. For the next few weeks I meditated twice daily and began to make connections with my dad in spirit each evening. Daddy had passed away in November 1999.This was utterly fantastic. I love my father so much and I had grieved for him and missed him for so long. Now he was here with me again every night and I could feel his energy, sometimes see him and I could hear the messages he gave to me. Well if I thought my life was blessed before now, how was that? Because, it was well and truly blessed now. My soul felt more alive than ever, as if it had suddenly found purpose! The sun shined brighter and my heart surged with unconditional love for everyone and everything. My gratitude list was expanding all the time and my prayer time getting longer. I truly have so much to be thankful for.

On Sunday 10th May I woke early and was full of the joys of life. After a guided meditation I then sat in silence for a time. I asked my spirit guide to give me a sign that she could hear me. I asked her for a feather. I then stood up and began to tidy the sitting room. I brought a glass out to the kitchen and I returned an angel to the dining room. When I entered the dining room I saw the feather on the ground right in front of the table I was about to put the angel back on. Wow that was fast! I stood there in amazement. It was a beautiful white feather. I picked it up and wondered how it really happened, I thought it might be possible but I was not sure until right now. Ask and you shall receive! Oh me oh my, I was beyond excited!

My spirit guide is also called Jane; she is also my great grandmother on my father's side of the family. She revealed herself to me almost a year ago! That evening I was sitting on my usual place on the couch, when the sun glared through the window and was blinding me. It usually did not get to me in this seat so I thought it a bit strange. I was guided to go outside so I grabbed my phone on the way out, just incase I wanted to take a photograph. The sun was setting when I got outside and it was the most beautiful sky I had seen in my entire life up until that moment! I stayed in the moment and soaked in the beauty and magnificence of this world God has created. It was spectacular! I took some photographs and then I went and sat and watched the sun go down. Later on when I looked back on the photos they were all full of spirit activity. They were totally amazing! There was the most awesome sky, spirit faces in the trees, heart shaped clouds and heavenly rays of angelic light shining down from above. I was so thankful for being guided outside to experience such beauty and blessings. Thank you, thank you, and thank you!

The rest of the month was pretty much taken up with work and practicing my communication with spirit and the angels. On Saturday 30th May, Mike was in our bedroom and he stepped into the hallway and called me to go down there to him. I finished what I was doing and I went down to him. On my dresser I have a little alter and one of the items on it is a Giant Amethyst. Mike said to me "Look at the Amethyst and tell me what you can see". I looked at it and to my surprise and amazement I could see my dad's face smiling back at me! I said to Mike "I see my dad, how is this happening?" Mike replied "I don't know but it is awesome, it must take an awful lot of energy to manifest an image up there though". We sat on the edge of the bed and kept examining the amethyst. We marveled when we saw Mike's mum appear, our son Patrick and so many other faces of our loved ones in spirit. This was absolutely mind blowing! I felt we really have no idea who was surrounding us and helping us the entire time. The world just got bigger!

CHAPTER 3

Guided Adventures

On a Tuesday after dinner on the 9th June I sat outside in the evening sunshine to meditate. Mike had created a stone circle around a tree at the side of the house and I love to sit in there, the energy is very high there. I had brought my phone out too and put on a meditation to meet your spirit guide. As I relaxed into this meditation, my main guide Jane connected to me and then another lady connected to me. The new lady told me her name was Maya and I could see she was a Native American. I could sense that changes were about to happen for me as my new guide would help me with new tasks. I wondered what these changes could be.

The following week on a Tuesday evening I took my position in the stone circle to meditate with my spirit guide again. As I relaxed into the meditation, Jane connected and then Maya connected with me. Then I had a new connection come through and it was a male. He introduced himself as Prometheus from Greece. Then he said to me "continue to learn as the benefits will be great". Wow this was awesome, all these spirit guides full of wisdom, I was blessed and feeling the love! I had never heard the name Prometheus so I looked it up on the internet. I read that Prometheus was a Greek God. This was mad stuff! I could not make this up, even in my wildest dreams.

I started practicing my medium ship for Mike a few evenings a week around now. My connections were good but I needed to strengthen them and keep them longer by practicing more. Mikes family members in spirit were fantastic to me, helping me to train and learn. The noise in my right ear became very strong around now and I was receiving vast amounts of divine messages in downloads from the universe too. Sometimes it sounded like a train going through a tunnel the level of energy flowing into my right ear!

On Saturday July 18th I was in the shop and I was just after polishing the counter and I was standing there admiring the great job I had done. Next thing that happened was this very bright white large circle of light came down from the ceiling and flew in towards my face, and then it rose upwards and floated down to the shop. It then disappeared through the wall! I was filled with an intense feeling of peace and love as I had watched this angel energy float around me. In that moment Mike walked into the shop and said "Hello, you look like you just saw God!" I replied" I think I just saw an actual angel".

I began to tell Mike what had just happened and he found the story was as amazing as I did. He went to the camera video recorder and rewound it to a few minutes before and we waited until the bright light appeared. We were speechless as we both watched, while it did its dance through our shop and then go out through the wall. Incredible! And to have it on camera was awesome. When I told my friends they didn't think I was crazy or imagining things at all!

On August 18th Mike and I sat out in an teach (The healing house, Mike and his brother had built it for me last Christmas, it is shaped like a pyramid and has awesome healing energy in there) to meditate. I lit incense before we started and we did a nice long meditation, we then decided to go into the house and sit in the dining room. The incense had not burned out and I did not want to let it lighting while we were not in the healing house so I decided to take it in with us and place it in a holder on my little angel table in the dining room. I had hung some solar powered lights in the window and the room was beautiful at night. Mike brought both of us a glass of water and we sat in candlelight sipping our water and chatting. I then noticed a lot of smoke coming from the incense stick and thought that's so strange because there was only a small bit of a stick not burnt when I brought it in from outside. I got my phone to take a picture, to see if anything of angel or a spirit nature would show up.

It was amazing to watch the smoke rise and fall, swirl left and then right, it was forming magical shapes. Mike and I sat and watched it for about thirty minutes! It was a magnificent sight, how could that tiny stick make so much smoke and how was it dancing before our eyes? When the smoke stopped and the incense was burnt out, I turned on the light so we could look at the pictures and see if we could get a clue as to what had just happened. I opened the gallery on my phone and the first picture I saw was a beautiful face looking out at me, from a haze of incense smoke. It was my guide Jane, I knew her straight away! Thank you Jane. I had recently asked Jane if there was any photograph of her I could get my hands on for my family tree, as I did already have one of her husband William! I had found the picture of Old Bill (as he was known) on an internet genealogy site posted by an American lady whose father was from Kerry last year! Wow, now I had one of Jane too! I felt so excited and I felt so connected with Jane, more than I had ever been before. I said "Jane you are awesome". This was just magical! I was feeling so blessed.

A few days later I was in the shop with my son Nathan, when an American lady walked in, she saw my sign for Angel card Readings and she began to cry, through her tears she said "Thank God, I had asked the angels for help and here you are"." I had only come into this centre to buy milk! "I went to the other side of the counter and spoke quietly with her and we agreed that she would come in for a reading in half a hour. I asked Nathan if he would cover the shop while I did the reading and he said he would. I then went and set up my little reading room for my client.

When I had the room ready I sat and did a quick grounding and meditation, I had a feeling this would be a tough session. I asked the angels for their help to heal this lady who was clearly very emotional. As I had felt before her reading, it was a very intense session which was very emotional for my client on many levels. A lot from her past had resurfaced as she walked the land of her grandparents for the first time. When Lillian was calmer and received her angel's guidance we hugged as we said our goodbyes. My hand chakras activated as soon as I touched her and I knew she was receiving intense healing at this moment. We remained in this hug for three to four minutes. When we let go of each other she looked so different, she looked younger and all the stress had been removed from her face, she had the biggest smile and then Lillian said "thank you so much Jane, you have changed my life." She was extremely grateful and feeling very positive when she left. I prayed to God that she would in fact have an easier life after today and I thanked the angels for their loving and divine wisdom.

The very next morning I pulled up the shutter door in the shop. There were five black and grey feathers laying in a row in front of the counter. All lined up from smallest to largest in that order. I knew these had something to do with the lady I had read for yesterday, such a powerful healing had taken place, but as to what it could mean I had no idea. I got out my angel book and I looked for color feather meanings. Deep spiritual growth was what these feathers signified and because there was five that message was magnified. I felt so overjoyed, bring it on I thought! Blessed are we.

In my dining room window hangs a sun catcher, it is made up of five purple and red glass hearts, small ones on top and a larger heart on the bottom. They hang one below the other and it is a beautiful piece. Four days after I received the five feathers, I was sitting in the dining room when the sun catcher started to move. I watched it as it swayed over and back, over and back. How was this happening?, there was no door or window open to cause it to move. It was mesmerizing to watch it spin. Nothing either side of it moved. We are surrounded by beautiful angels, life is beautiful! That evening when Mike was home I told him to watch the sun catcher in the dining room. He was blown away by it.

The next day after we had eaten dinner, Mike went outside to feed the animals. I was in the sitting room when he returned to the back door; he did not come in but shouted for me to go outside. I thought he might want to show me the beautiful sunset so I grabbed my phone off the island on my way past. When I got outside Mike was standing in front of the utility window and he said to me "look at my reflection and tell me what you see". I looked in the window and was shocked to see the reflection was not Mike's? How was this possible and what was going on? "Who is that" I said to Mike, and Mike replied "I have no idea!" We pondered over these questions as Mike moved nearer and further, to and from the window. Then Mike suggested I try it, so I did. I stepped in front of the window and the reflection was not me. This is such a strange thing to experience. I moved my face and stuck out my tongue and the image did the same but it was not me! This was beyond strange! We must have played around like this for an hour before going back inside. After discussing what it could be, we decided it must be our spirit guides and left it at that! I had taken some photographs while we were outside and I emailed them to a friend of mine who was also a medium.

She said it was transfiguration. What on earth is that I asked her? She responded it is when spirit superimposes their image onto a mediums' face. She had studied it in a course earlier in the year. How cool was that? I thought it was super cool! I was still wondering why it happened, who it was and for what reason did it happen? I wasn't afraid in any way by this occurrence, in actual fact I felt totally blessed. I knew on some level it would all make sense someday. The five hearts sun catcher continues to turn every day and is so mesmerizing and peaceful to watch. I was wondering who was moving it and it began to stay on my mind those days. I thought it might be my dad or my guide or the angels, I really did not know.

One evening in late August I sat in meditation in the dining room and as I opened my eyes afterward the hearts were turning so I closed my eyes again. I called on my spirit guide Jane and I asked her "who is turning those hearts and why are they being turned?" Jane answered me straight away and in my internal ear I heard her say "we are turning them for you, and I am showing you a little of the great love that is here for you".

My heart swelled with such emotion at hearing these beautiful words. I said "Thank you Jane and thank you to all my loved ones in spirit who help to turn those hearts every day."Oh my God I felt such an overwhelming gratitude for all the love I felt from my loved ones in spirit, from the angels, the archangels, the saints and God. The five heart sun catcher continues to turn to this day. Blessed be.

Earlier in the summer Mike had hurt his chest, when pulling a small tree from the ground to replant it elsewhere in the garden. He had been to the doctor a few times and was in terrible pain at times. He had been referred to the county hospital and had a scan done. On September 9th Mike received a referral letter to a specialist in Cork University hospital for another scan as the last scan was not detailed enough. We both felt things might be a bit more serious than we thought initially, when he was being sent for tests on better scanning machines in a different county now.

We sat in the dining room and I lit a few candles. We sat in meditation for some time. We did a powerful healing with the angel's meditation which was absolutely beautiful. We talked for a while and decided that whatever was wrong with Mike we would trust in God that everything would work out for our highest good. We were having a drink and a general chit chat about our day when I noticed the Buddha tea light holder on the table. The tea light within the holder had become very smoky. I had never seen a smoky tea light before! I said to Mike "Buddha is sending smoke signals tonight ". We both laughed and turned our attention to the tea light .The candle spluttered three times and then the flame rose high up and danced around the sides of the holder. It burned so brightly, danced, shone and heated for the next two hours. It was magical to watch it, so calming and captivating. When it finally burned out the inside of the metal holder was totally black with no sign of any wax from the candle left in it as would usually be there! I said to Mike " This is a special message for you that anything is possible and everything will work out fine no matter what the scan results reveal". This resonated strongly with Mike himself and he was overwhelmed with the beauty of the sign he received with this message.

I began to give Mike reiki two or three times a week from that day. Mike was now feeling well but had a lot of on going tests in the pipeline. After working in the shop one day in September, I was driving home when I thought of my little angel in Heaven. I silently said "Patrick I know you can hear me and are always with me, but can you give me a physical sign that you have heard this. I would love some communication with you, please make it a big sign as I'm driving and don't want to miss it "At that moment my phone binged, a text had come in. I said to myself I'll check that when I get home and kept an eye on the sky for a sign from my little angel.

I arrived home and thought I must have missed the sign, as I hadn't seen anything that I thought could be a sign. I went inside and looked at my phone. The text was from Nathan, it read "Hi mom, what's going on? I am in a car travelling down from county Meath and the sun is on the right side of the car. I am sitting in the left back and as I was looking out the window the brightest light came down out of the clouds and then a hand appeared and waved at me!" I knew this was my sign from Patrick, my heart and eyes filled with tears, as I text Nathan back and said "I will explain to you when you get home". I felt that I must be missing the signs Patrick sends me, so that is why Nathan received it in order to tell me about it.

Bless you Patrick my sweet angel and bless you Nathan for the ability to receive this miraculous sign. Mike was not at home that evening, he was helping his brother with a job. He was not home by the time I put the children to bed, so I spent a little longer on story time than I usually would. I had not told him of the sign I had asked Patrick for and received. It was dark when I came back down from upstairs and when I walked into the sitting room Mike was sitting there in the dark. I got the fright of my life! Mike said that the turbo was gone on his car and he would not be able to work without it. He asked me to go out to his car and press the accelerator while he tried to reconnect a pipe underneath the car. Out we went and did that and Mike said he would take the car for a test drive and come back and let me know how it went. Mike drove off and I went inside to warm up.

Around five minutes later Mike returned and said "I was going to ring you",then I said "it didn't work?" and he replied "oh yes hon, it did but you are not going to believe what I am about to tell you. I was driving down to the crossroads when I saw a rainbow of angel light at the end of the road and as I drove through it, the most amazing feeling came over me. I knew this was special so I drove on to test the car and returned to the crossroad as soon as I could. The rainbow of angel light was still there, just at the end of our road. As I drove under it again I decided I would bring you down to see it. I looked in my rear view mirror and it was gone." I said "oh wow that sounds magical and so beautiful. That was from Patrick". Mike said "how do you know that, you seem so sure". I sat down and told him all about Patrick and Nathan earlier in the evening. I knew then in my heart that I miss the signs my baby gives me so he gave them to the two men in the house to make sure I got them. Bless you Patrick and thank you from deep within my soul. And thank you God for the magic all around us.

September 17th is my dad's birthday. I went to a shop after work and decided to bring some roses to the graveyard on my way home. There was a choice of red, pink and yellow roses. They were all so beautiful. First I was getting the red ones, but the pink were beautiful, I was humming and hawing over them for ages, when I finally said to myself pick the yellow ones so I did! Nathan was with me as we drove to the graveyard. When we got to the grave we said our few prayers. We then began to tidy up and place the yellow roses there. Nathan jokingly said "can you make it rain granddad we need water for your flower!" Just then I saw a jar with water in it behind his headstone so I said "false alarm daddy, no need for rain". We put the roses in the jar and they were stunning. We both sat for a while in private repose and I told daddy how much I missed him. We said some more prayers before leaving. It had not rained while we were there. On the drive home, just as I was turning right off the main road, Nathan said " do you remember the rain I asked granddad for that we never got " I said "yes " and Nathan said " good, because it just made the biggest brightest, most colorful rainbow of all time! I looked to my right and we both said in unison "Wow, Oh my God! " It was the most spectacular rainbow! It stayed with us for the last few miles, to our house.

When I pulled into our driveway the rainbow appeared to be over our garden! I drove behind the house and the rainbow was so low just above the garage. We jumped out of the car and I called out to the Hannah and Michael to come outside to see the giant rainbow. I took some photographs but they really didn't do it justice. We were all amazed by its vibrancy and rich colours. Standing outside looking up at it we began naming the colours, it was truly a magical moment. Thank you daddy, you are awesome! Later on that evening after I finished my nightly meditation I asked daddy why did I eventually choose the yellow roses, were they a favourite of his? He replied "you are my yellow rose of Texas ". I laughed at this and just then a memory filled my mind of me as a young girl and daddy singing that song to me as I sat on his lap. He used to change the lyrics and make up his own to suit me. Bless you daddy, you are the best, and I love you. I had a little cry and then went off to bed.

A few days later I was giving Mike a healing session in the dining room, I had the therapy bed set up in there. I placed some crystals at his shoulder and his feet. I called on Archangel Raphael to assist me in this healing and to shine his healing light on Mike for the entire session. The heat transmitting from Mike's body was incredible throughout the session. As I was working on Mike, when I got to his sacral chakra I thought he had his hands on his chest as I could see a big lump under the blanket. I thought this strange as he knew he should have his hands by his sides. I continued to work around the lump and finished the session in an hour.

Afterwards I walked to the kitchen sink to wash my hands, when Mike said to me" can I sit up now?" I was puzzled as to why he was asking me that as there was no reason he could not sit up. I replied "yes, why not?" Mike replied "must you take some stone from my chest first?" I said "no, I didn't put anything on your chest". Mike sat up and we were both drinking a glass of water whilst discussing his healing session. Mike was convinced that I had placed an egg shaped crystal on his chest and at times it was very uncomfortable and he thought of asking me to take it off but he reasoned that I had put it there for a reason so he would put up with it. I agreed with him about the size of the lump I had seen on the blanket. We were both pondering in amazement at what had happened. It was absolutely incredible! Mike then had an intense pain on his right side near his ribs and he looked very pale. I instinctively knew he was going through an intense healing so I suggested he take it easy for the next few days. Every night there were angel orbs in the dining room after I meditated in there. I was actively and consistently meditating every morning and night now and loving it. I was feeling blessed!

CHAPTER 4

The Healing House (An Teach)

Michael had eczema as a baby and every so often he would get a flare up. On October 5ᵗʰ Michael was up early for school and I was helping him to get dressed. I noticed his right leg was scratched raw and was bleeding a little and his left leg was riddled with rash. I walked to the kitchen to get his eczema cream when on the way I stopped in my tracks and I heard" What are you doing? You can heal him yourself; if he has a rash there is an internal problem. Treat it holistically ".

I made up a cream with essential oils to salve his poor legs and applied it straight away to stop the itch. After work I lay him on the therapy bed and laid my hands on him for about five minutes. He would not lie still for any longer. The next morning when I went to apply the cream his legs were about 70 percent better, I was amazed. That evening after work, I again laid him on the therapy bed and placed my hands on him for only four minutes, he did not want to stay so I let it at that. The next morning when I went to apply the cream I had made, to his legs, I got a shock, they were better! Both legs healed. His left leg had no rash, beautiful clear smooth skin and his right shin which had been bleeding two days ago was a match except for a tiny mark like a beauty spot near his knee! Oh My God! This was amazing! That evening after work I checked Michael's legs and both were 100 percent healed. I called Mike to come have a look at Michael's legs and he could not believe how they had healed so fast. I felt excited and anxious when I said to Mike "I must share this, it is wrong not to share this with people when so many people are suffering". Mike said "Absolutely, you have a gift, you must use it."

The next morning I went in to the shop and I had an hour free before my first client for a reading of the day. I decided it was time for me to come out of the spiritual closet and own up to who I am. So I logged in to face book and created a post saying that I am a Reiki Master and a Certified Angel Card Reader. It may seem hard to believe, but I had not told anyone when I did my reiki course as I did not feel they would be open to it, and as for angel card reading I thought they might find me odd, or weird! So now putting myself out there I clicked post, Angels please continue to guide me I prayed.

It was just about two hours later when the phone rang and it was a friend of mine that I hadn't seen in years. She had seen my post and that very morning she had asked God for help, she needed a sign. When she logged on to her face book my post was the first she saw and she thought, Thank you God! Her family was experiencing great difficulties at the time so she booked a session for two days later. I was thrilled; I had not expected a job so soon! Later on when I got time to go back onto face book I was amazed by the likes and comments my post had received. So many messages of well wishes and luck. Such support was overwhelming, my heart filled with gratitude and I felt blessed to have such friends. Eek, I was going to have my very first client for a healing, whoopee! The next day I was busy in the morning with readings and in the afternoon I was at home. I decided to get An Teach ready and turn it from my private meditation room into a healing room. This purpose built pyramid shape one room house was built in my garden, completed in March 2015. The Christmas before Mike said to me in early November "what do you want for Christmas?" I replied "what I really want is a house outside of this house where I can sit in peace and quietness! "Mike thought this was a great idea and took it on board with a passion.

Both Mike and his brother Dan were working full time jobs so the hours they could work together were very limited. Through wind rain and storms they worked through, until the beginning of March until completion. Every morning for the next six months or so I get up earlier and came out here to sit in meditation before I went back inside the house to wake the children for school. I also came out here every night for half an hour, when the children went to bed. The time I spent here in solitude, meditation and prayer was heavenly and it was the food my soul needed. The energy in the pyramid was amazing and when I researched it online I learnt that we could charge the water we drink in there for a multitude of benefits! I certainly was feeling on top of the world and thriving and spiritually growing with each experience I had in this special healing place.

Mike helped me to carry out and set up the therapy bed inside the healing house and we were absolutely amazed when it fitted in perfectly! I was so excited that I had a client the next day and I knew in my heart that with Gods help, I could help her with her life. The healing room looked amazing and yes it was perfect with a bed, two chairs, a salt lamp, a giant amethyst, candles and some more little pieces to finish of the desired relaxed effect. That evening Mike and I sat in there for a gratitude meditation. There were two beautiful orbs floating around the room. I felt so blessed in that moment and I knew I was on the right path and new doors would be opening for me very soon. I felt excited and giddy, I love helping others and now I would be helping people to tap into their own inner healing. Life is such a blessing!

On October 11th I had my first non family member in an teach (my healing house). Nuala arrived a few minutes early and we had a nice chat as she settled in. Nuala loved the room and said it felt so cozy and homely in there. She lay on the bed and I tucked her in with a warm blanket around her .I explained a little on energy healing and told her I would be working with the angels and with reiki on her. She said "oh that sounds beautiful, I desperately need something." She became relaxed very quickly and as I had my hands on her head I saw a beautiful white angel orb in the right corner of the room. It is wonderful to feel protected by the angels in this way. I intuited problems with her throat, her ovaries, her right knee and her heart chakra was put of balance. When we spoke afterwards she was amazed at how relaxed she felt and how beautiful the entire experience was. Nuala told me she was going through some issues with her ovaries and having scans done at the moment. She had unprocessed grief which was her heart chakra problem, her throat related to the trauma that was going on with her family and she had hurt her knee, playing ladies football. I was amazed and delighted I had picked up so much from her and knew she received a good healing. She told me about the issues at home and a little about her unprocessed grief which made total sense to me and my heart went out to her. My admiration grew for her also as she was battling through tough days and keeping her head well above water. She would realize this some day soon, how proud she should be of herself but just now she felt she was not good enough at any of it. Bless her. She could not get over how good she felt as she was leaving and I felt so happy for her. I cleaned down the room and brushed out the floor. I then knelt and prayed for her, Nuala is such a wonderful lady and I prayed for her family, they were experiencing such a deeply personal issue and it was having devastating effects on more than one family member, which was bringing extreme stress to all of the family.

The next morning I was up with the lark, full of the joys of life. I went in to the shop and did the shop work that needed attention first. I then designed some business cards online and ordered my very first business cards, this felt so good! I was feeling so inspired. I then created some flyers on my computer advertising my healing services. I hung one inside my shop and one outside on the window. Nathan called in later that day and took some flyers to put up in other businesses in town.

Within and hour I had a client booked in for healing tomorrow. Whoopee, I was so born to do this! This was so amazing. It was another amazing session and this lady Sabrina had such compliments for me I was feeling a bit uncomfortable with all the praise coming my way. I certainly was not used to such amazing positive feedback. I thanked God for these gifts he has given me so that I can help other beautiful souls to heal. I have had clients for healing almost every working day since then. On October 22nd Mike's aunt and godmother Sheila passed away. She had been ill for some time and was a great age. We stood in the dining room and I lit a candle for Sheila. Then we both said some prayers for her soul. I asked Mike to hold the candle as I could feel spirit presence in the room and thought it may be Sheila. I went and got my phone so I could take a picture as the light was low and I could not see any angel orb with my naked eye but would with the camera tonight. As I held up my phone to take the picture Mike's jumper started flashing. It was very strange to watch. He was wearing a blue jumper with white strips and the blue and white appeared to be moving places! I took a few photos. I then said to Mike "keep a hold of the candle as I want to take a video, there is some strange activity here". He gave me a puzzled look but did as I asked anyway. In the video the most beautiful white orb flew past Mike. Then it flew around the room and did it again before it vanished! Mike and I had no doubt but it was Sheila and Mike found great comfort in this. He was absolutely amazed when he watched the video back later on that night it was such a special moment for Mike and his aunt on the evening of her passing into non physical. I was meditating a few mornings later when I heard these words in guidance "teach a meditation class". I thought about this for some time after and thought what an awesome idea it was! I researched on what type of class I would do and what meditations and exercises I would include. I printed out information sheets for the students and made up a program for my own use. I was super excited.

Wednesday November 18ᵗʰ was the first of five classes in the meditation group. I was holding them in the shop after the shop closed for the day. There were five ladies booked in for the class. All very different individuals, with very different lives and stresses. But they were united in one common goal, to have more peace in their lives. Every class was amazing and we enjoyed it so much meditating together. It was wonderful to see the changes in each of these ladies as they begun practicing meditation. I felt so proud of each of them; the desire to improve their lives was so admirable! The five weeks flew past and the course was over before we knew what had happened. I was so thankful for this opportunity and blessed to make some new wonderful lasting friendships also.

On Friday 20th November early in the morning I sat in meditation and had a wonderful strong connection with my spirit guide Jane. We were able to have a conversation which was beautiful! I asked Jane to send me a sign; I would love something in the physical, please and thank you! I worked the shop all day and forgot about asking for a sign from Jane. I went outside to lock up the shutters of the shop to close up for the evening. I opened the zip pocket of my handbag where the shop keys sit all day once the shop is open. When I took the keys out there was a black feather intertwined in the keys and all knotted in them. I thought how did that get there and carried on locking up.

I totally forgot about the feather until the next morning, it then dawned on me this was the sign from Jane I had asked for! Oh God I felt awful. I apologized to Jane for not noticing and recognizing the beautiful sign she had given me. I went to take a picture of the beautiful feather and I asked her again for a sign today and I promised I would pay more attention this time! Off I went into town and headed for the shop to open it up for the day unlocked the first shutter and pulled it up until it slid to the top and then I noticed the feather! It was right inside the door, I could not possibly miss it. I thought Jane you are awesome, thank you it's beautiful. The feather was brown with some green near the tip, it was very unusual. I was intrigued to know what those colors signified so I powered on the computer. My book was at home and I could not wait all day to find out.

Brown feathers signify grounding, home life and stability, and a balance between physical and spiritual. Green feathers signify abundance and money. This was such a beautiful message from Jane, as well as good health, well being and love. Oh wow I was delighted with my spirit guide and I am blessed beyond words to receive such loving guidance and to understand it. Around this time I was actively connecting to spirit daily. Different days I would work with different family members in spirit. My dad, my brother, my nanas, my granddads, uncles, aunts ...... It was awesome and I loved and cherished these special moments. To feel the love from beyond the grave is the most beautiful intense emotion that I cannot give words to describe it adequately.

On Sunday 6ᵗʰ December we put up our Christmas decorations. Hannah and Michael were so excited and were putting tinsel everywhere but mostly wearing it! We had such fun pulling ornaments and things out of boxes and finding the right spot for them. Mike put up the tree and I helped him put the lights on it. Drama free and no knotted lights! Thank you angels! It really was a blissful morning. The little ones hung the decorations on the tree after lunch. They stretched as far and as high up as they could. I finished off the top where they could not reach and it looked amazing. We all love Christmas so I thought let the excitement begin!

I asked Hannah and Michael to stand in front of the tree so that I could take a photograph. I took some beautiful photos and it was amazing to see how much they each had grown since last Christmas. You really do notice time passing and these things more with children that we do with ourselves. When I looked at the photographs after, they were not blurred in any way, but Hannah did not look like Hannah and Michael did not look like Michael! I zoomed in and out, it was amazing. On the out zoom they looked like themselves and on the in zoom they looked nothing like themselves, ah its transfiguration I thought. The next evening I asked Mike to stand in the same place in front of the tree and I took some photographs of him. I was dying to see if the transfiguration would occur again. I was not disappointed; yes it did occur again! what did all this mean? And what was the message in it? It did not bother me or upset me in the slightest but I was really curious as to know what spirit was trying to tell me!

The following Wednesday was the day of the school Christmas Play .It was being held in a local hotel at 8 pm tonight .Both Hannah and Michael had been practicing songs for the past few weeks and the excitement was at fever pitch! I was driving both of them to school when Hannah said to me "mom I'm feeling nervous". I said "ah pet, there is no need for nerves, just feel the excitement, asks your guardian angel to help calm your nerves. Your guardian angel can help you with anything, just ask." I then said "Close your eyes and take in two slow deep breaths, breathing in peace and breathing out nerves." Hannah then opened her eyes and said "What is my angels name; how can I talk to her if I don't know her name?" I replied " Some day when you have time, at home you can sit in your room and ask your guardian angel her name but for now just do the slow breaths, close your eyes and ask for what you need right now. Hannah replied "I need my legs to not get sore tonight is what I need". She then closed her eyes and as I looked in my rear view mirror her hands were held in prayer and her eyes were squeezed shut. Bless her, she looked so beautiful! I thought. Hannah then excitedly said "She told me her name, at least I think that's her name, it's strange, is there even such a name as Muriel? She is very pretty with light colored hair and has plaits going round the side of her head." I replied "yes Hannah, there is in fact an angel Muriel "and I was both delighted and surprised to have heard this. Then Hannah said "there are no messer angels are there mom?" I answered her that angels are always kind and nice and are always good. Hannah said "because Muriel is laughing and laughing, is she laughing at me?" I said "Oh no Hannah, she is not laughing at you, she is laughing because she is delighted to know you and now you will be asking her for help with things. You should be laughing at this too princess! Then Hannah laughed too. I reminded her to ask Muriel to calm her nerves. Hannah replied "I don't have to mom, I am perfectly calm already! "I continued driving to the school and marveled at that whole conversation. I dropped the two off and gave them each a big hug, and with a kiss I left them at the gate of the school.

Before I opened the shop that morning I sat quietly in the back, in my little angel reading room. I said to myself if Hannah can connect to her guardian angel so easily, maybe so could I.I sat and took a few slow deep breaths to calm and centre myself. I then asked silently "Guardian Angel please tell me your name". The next word I heard in my mind was a male voice that said "Barrachiel". Wow oh wow this was amazing! Absolutely mind-blowing easy! It is so easy to hear our guardian angels and I have only discovered it through my beautiful daughter. I had never heard the word Barrachiel in my life so I wrote it down on a piece of paper along with the word Muriel to check on the internet later in the day. I went and opened the shop and focused on the tasks that needed my attention's, took a break at 11am and made myself a cup of green tea with lemon. It was my favorite drink at the moment. I sat down and began to feel very excited. I first searched for Angel Muriel; I learned that Archangel Muriel calms emotions with unconditional love and compassion. She will help anyone who calls on her but especially anyone struggling with emotions! There was a picture of her and OH My God she was exactly as Hannah had described her!

I saved the writing and the picture and I printed it out for Hannah, she would be thrilled. I then looked up Angel Barrachiel and found out that he is known as God's blessing. He is linked to Pisces, which is my astrological sign and the month of February (my birthday month).He is the chief angel of the guardian angels. I read this beautiful prayer to Archangel Barrachiel so I wrote it down. "Barrachiel, Angel of blessings. I thank God for making you a generous channel through which God pours many blessings into people's lives. Please intercede in prayer for me in all areas of my life-from my relationships with family and friends to my work. Grant me success in all of my pursuits, that line me up with Gods will for me. Teach me to understand blessings from an accurate perspective. Amen.

I was absolutely amazed at what I had read; I had one awesome guardian angel and so did my daughter Hannah! I could not wait until Mike heard this, it would blow his mind. After school time Mike, Hannah and Michael came into the shop. After asking how their days went I made them a snack. I then grabbed the print out of Hannah's angel I had done earlier and hid it behind my back. I then said to Hannah "Do you remember Muriel your angel you saw this morning "? She replied "yes" and with that I took the paper from behind my back and showed it to her. Hannah got very excited and jumped up and down as she pointed at Archangel Muriel and screeched "That is her!" I kneeled down on the ground and gave Hannah a big hug. I then read to her all the lovely things about her special angel. What a special day that was. The school concert went off brilliantly that night and not a nerve in sight by Hannah thankfully! The show was fantastic;

all the students made us parents very proud. The next few weeks on the run up to Christmas were busy with the shop and clients.

Mike had received another appointment for December 21ˢᵗ to go to Cork University Hospital to get the results of the blood work and scans taken last month. I would not be able to go with him as we had no one to mind the two little ones if only we had someone to work the shop. We discussed bringing them with us but felt a hospital that size was no place for children when they did not have to be there. Mike was happy to go on his own so we agreed that is what he would do. The night before I gave Mike a reiki healing which he found greatly relaxed him, I knew he was a little anxious about his results and I wanted him to get a good night's sleep. He always sleeps sound after a healing from me. Mike had an early start so we both got up early and I made him some breakfast. He told me he would ring me as soon as he could today. When it was time for him to go I called on Archangel Michael to protect him and make this day as easy as it could be for Mike. We hugged and with a kiss, off he went on that long drive to the hospital. It was too early to call the children for their last day of school before Christmas, so I decided to go out to my healing house and meditate to take my mind off the day's events. My guide Jane connected to me and told me everything is as it should be. I deeply valued this guidance and thought yes I trust that God has a plan and we as a family will be fine. I then went inside and woke the children and off to school and work we went. I wasn't in the shop long when I got such a dread in my stomach, all that morning I felt it and I did not know why, please God, there would be no bad news from the hospital. My phone rang just after half past twelve and I saw it was Mike. With fingers crossed I answered it and say "Hi Mike how did that go"?

CHAPTER 5

Testing Times

Mike said he was on his way home, he was connected to his Bluetooth device and driving down from Cork. I thought that all sounds good. Then Mike said "I have cancer sweetheart "My heart skipped a beat. I replied "I was not expecting to hear that news sweetheart but we will overcome this, so try not to worry". He began to tell me how it went .There was the consultant and a nurse in the room when Mike entered it and he then sat down. The consultant said "the news is not good Mike; have you anyone here with you today"? Mike said he told them that I was minding the children and working in the shop, so he decided to come alone. Mike was informed he had cancer in his right lung and it was in his bones as well. He was told he must have had it for a long time because it was very advanced in his bones and there was nothing could be done for it now. An operation was not an option.

Mike asked the doctor what time frame had he left and the doctor said it's hard to put a time on these things but it could be six months. The consultant returned to Mikes notes and noted that he had two very young children. He then spoke to the nurse and recommended a term of chemotherapy to try an elongate Mike's life. He told Mike he would start him on a course of Chemotherapy to give him some more time, It may go from 6 months to a year or so. It would be impossible to say.

As I listened to Mike relaying this to me I thought "Dear Lord Help us", and I asked Archangel Michael to give me the strength and courage I needed to remain strong for Mike. I remained calm as Mike spoke and I said reassuring words that I don't now remember. We spoke of miracle healings that we had read about, Anita Moorjani and Dr Wayne Dyer among other stories. We decided then and there that Mike would get his miracle too. After the phone call I went into shock. I was in no way prepared for news of this scale. I began to cry, my poor little children might grow up without their dad that they love and adore so much. Me without my awesome husband....How tragic would that be? I wallowed in misery for a few minutes. I then said to myself "stop this self pity, Mike can't fight this alone. I have to be stronger than him to keep his faith strong and raise him up when he needs it." I stopped crying and I prayed to God for the extra faith we both would need. I prayed to Archangel Raphael for special healing for Mike. I prayed to Archangel Michael for the strength and wisdom I would need for as long as I would need it. I then thanked them all for their presence in my life and the invaluable guidance and support they give to me. By the time I saw Mike that evening I had a healing strategy in place and we would not dwell on the cancer but on wellbeing, healing and health. Mike welcomed this positive pro active attitude, with an open heart and an open mind.

The next day Mike began his Reiki treatments for one hour each session. I allotted space in my diary for his healings every second day or every day when needed. I bought him some book with positive affirmations for healing his heart. The lungs are related to the heart chakra .I made him cds with healing rampages on them, to listen to when he was in the car. I made him a cd mix of meditations for healing, for him to listen to also. We were aiming to give Mike a more positive mindset as he healed himself. Mike wanted to keep this news to ourselves until after Christmas, as we did not want to upset anyone so close to the Christmas. We put the cancer out of our minds and focused on all the positive changes and aspects we could and live day by day. We had a wonderful Christmas and the children never knew dad was sick.

On Tuesday January 6th 2016 I was giving Mike an angel healing and using crystals' to magnify the healing when Mikes mum appeared to me and connected with me just like a spirit guide would. It was a little strange but it felt alright so I just relaxed with it. She placed her hands on Mike's toes using my hands and showed me an image of Mike as a baby, her youngest child and how she would sit at the end of the cot and hold his toes as she was doing now. It was such a beautiful love filled vision. After a little while Mike's mom faded away and his uncle, his granddad and his nana came through with messages for Mike.

Mike would begin his first round of chemotherapy tomorrow and his loved ones all had wonderful words of encouragement and love. It was a very powerful and emotional healing for Mike. They had told him not to worry, that everything would be just fine. A friend of mine worked the shop on the 6th January Mike had his chemotherapy appointment at 9.30 am. My friend that was working the shop for me, she was unaware of where Mike and I were going. Nathan looked after Hannah and Michael and he also did not know anything about it.

Mike was feeling confident and I thanked the angels and God for that. It would definitely make this day easier. Mike and I headed off to the hospital and the angels had saved a nice parking spot for us as I had requested. We went in to the waiting room that was filled with cancer patients of different levels of disease and treatments. I was overwhelmed by their pain. I mentally grounded myself and I prayed for them all, I did not know these people but I asked God to help each and every one of them. I was able to sit with Mike and hold his hand for a few hours until it was time for the chemotherapy drugs to be administered. I was then asked to wait in the waiting room for about four hours. Mike looked well when he returned to find me and it was time to go home, day one was down! Mike had managed to have a nap whilst the drugs were going into him by drip and he also managed to eat some lunch. He was in great form leaving the hospital. I said a silent prayer of thanks to God, the angels and everyone else I had prayed to. Mike could not have had a better day of treatments and that really can make all the difference on a day like that.

The next day Mike was a little tired but in good spirits. I reminded him to take things easy as he is always working too hard. That night Mike found it very hard to sleep and had terrible hiccups that went on for hours. I went and got a blanket from the spare room and I propped it under the mattress on Mike's side of the bed. I felt if he was not lying down flat he may get some relief, all those years I had worked in the nursing home in my early twenties were not a waste i thought. As Mike lay, half propped up the hiccups subsided and eventually stopped; Thank God he then slept for a while. The following morning Mike looked so pale and he was unable to eat for most of the day. As soon as he ate something in the afternoon those hiccups came back stronger than yesterday. It was torture to watch a man who has always been as strong as an ox, the man i love so much, so feeble and weak now. He spent most of the day in and out of little naps with no energy for anything at all. I bought him some digestive remedy to help with those hiccups and thankfully it worked through all the other chemotherapy treatments Mike received. I prayed and prayed those first days as I cared for Mike the best I could. Making sure he ate a little often and no big meals. I kept him warm, as he could get perished in a moment and had no energy to heat his body.

I was continuing the energy healing every two days which Mike was getting great benefit from. I thanked God that I had this gift, the skill and the ability to help my husband through his suffering. I was running on auto pilot these days, I really could not have got through it without the angels and God. I was in and out of the shop; I had clients for readings and healings. I had the children to look after, and keep them extra quiet when dad was not feeling at all well. On Friday January 15th Mike was experiencing numbness in his legs so I gave him a reiki treatment and focused extra attention with some crystals to relieve those symptoms. Thankfully Mike had a powerful energy release and the blood started to flow as normal in his legs. Any spare moment I had these days, I began to re read all the books on angels I owned. I felt so grateful for all the love and support from God, the archangels, the angels, Jesus, Mary, The Saints and our loved ones in spirit. I could feel their presence in my life every day. I sat one morning at 5 am and said" thank you all, you are simply amazing and I love each and every one of you .I am blessed because of you and that allows me to be a blessing to others".

On Wednesday January 26th Mike had his second round of Chemotherapy. I got up very early and did a deep grounding so I would not be absorbing other people's pain when I got to the hospital. Whilst meditating afterwards a message came to me, "God is in charge of my life and I trust his judgment and wisdom. All is as it should be". His appointment was at 9am and we both set off excited to be on number two of six treatments. We both felt sure that he would be healed by the time number six came by at the latest. This time the nurse said I was not allowed in with him today or in the future chemotherapy treatments, he would have to do it alone. I waited all day in the waiting room of the cancer unit. Thank God i could use the time wisely; I meditated and prayed for Mike's recovery to full health. I was happy I could do something even if I could not hold his hand.

The power of prayer and positive intentions is phenomenal. Mike got on very well with this round. We were armed with the hiccup remedy this time and Mike was proactive rather than reactive and had very little bother this time. Thank God! We were both scheduled to go To London on the weekend of January 29th and we hoped and prayed Mike would feel well enough to go. We were booked in to an intensive medium ship weekend in a College in London. Nathan moved back home for the weekend and looked after the little ones and a friend of mine worked the shop. The angels seemed to be working some magic, as Mike had no side effects for this round of chemotherapy and off to London we went We were both feeling so excited and this trip could not have come at a better time. We so badly needed a break from doctors, hospitals, chemotherapy and tablets. The flight from Cork went beautifully, and it was hassle free. It felt strange to be on an airplane without the children but we knew they were well looked after so we quickly relaxed. The College was not far from the airport so we had some lunch in the airport. We booked a taxi from the airport to the college and that took about twenty minutes drive to get there. The college looked so impressive and the gardens and grounds were beautiful. I could not believe I was there!

There was a big crowd in the small reception room when we went to book in. We were handed a form to fill out while we waited for our turn to be admitted into The College. The form was an assessment on what level of spirit activity and connections we had. I had very little confidence in my own abilities but I seemed to be ticking all the boxes. My friend Marcella who had been here before had told me when I booked the course that I would be amazed at how advanced I was when I actually got here; maybe she was right I thought. It finally came to our turn and we were booked in very quickly then. We were not staying in the main house but in the annex.

The garden house was a few minutes walk from the college through the lovely gardens. We walked there and let ourselves in the main door and quickly found our room. It was small and simple but perfect for us for the weekend. We were able to lie down and have a rest before our first meeting in the Great Hall with all the students and tutors. I connected to my guide Jane as I lay there and asked her to help me to be the best I could be. We were super excited walking back up the College and on entering the Hall was amazing. The energy was electric in there. It was explained to us that we would be broken up into groups according to our skill levels and we could find which tutor we were under on a sheet of paper outside after the meeting. Mike and I were on different groups just as we had suspected. Mike was on the beginners group and I was on the advanced. Oh my God this is really happening I thought. How did I get on the advanced list when I had only connected to spirit for family members and a few friends? Maybe it was because I see spirit as well I thought. I had zero confidence in myself.

We wished each other luck and agreed a meeting point for after class. Then we went our separate ways, Mike to this tutor and me the other end of the college to mine. Patricia was my tutor's name and she was a really lovely lady. The seats were placed in a circle and her seat was at the top. I took my seat, third from the top to the left of her. The seats quickly filled and there were twenty of us. Everyone looked so normal and friendly I thought as I sat there, Silently I said" thank you Angels and thank you Jane ".Patricia began to speak and said" I will start on this side of the room, (pointing in my direction) and I want a demonstration from all of you. If I pass you for some reason, maybe that you don't feel ready, I will be back to you". Oh My God I thought, what is a demonstration? What if I can't do it? I began to feel sick, what was I doing here, maybe I was put in the wrong group, and all these thoughts were flooding my brain. Patricia spoke again and said "You are all to participate unless the person doing the speaking is sitting next to you. Then you prepare yourself to receive spirit." Right I thought to myself, she is not passing me, I'm going to do this, this is what I came here for to learn and get rid of the fear.

The first person stood up and told us that she had a spirit connected to her; described the person and one of the other students put up their hand and said that is my mother. Some more details came through and it lasted about five minutes or so. I relaxed a little and thought I can do that, sure I had done it loads of times last year since I began practicing my medium ship and communicating with spirit and angels. The man next to me stood up and began to speak, I tuned out of the conversation and connected with my guide Jane and invited a spirit to join me for someone in the room. Just then I felt the spirit of a lovely quiet gentleman come close to me. Thank you

God! I thought as it was my turn to stand at the top of the room. I began to describe this lovely man and passed on any information he gave to me. A lady four seats away from me said it was her uncle. He had a beautiful message for her and she became emotional and cried, then I passed on some more information from him and she laughed. This was all making sense to her. He then told me how close they both had been and she agreed with this. I thanked her for accepting her uncle and silently I thanked her uncle for choosing me to be his voice .I was extremely grateful to him and I always smile when I think of him. I sat down and breathed the biggest sigh of relief in my life that was exhilarating, what had I been afraid of?

I was so happy to be here. It was fascinating to watch the other mediums work and the differences between us all were amazing. There were so many lovely and interesting people in my group and Patricia my tutor was awesome! A man stood up to have his turn and his connection was for me, it was my grandfather on my mother's side. The medium described my granddad to a tee; I did not doubt he was here in the room with us. He spoke of my confidence being shattered by a deceitful teacher and now it was time to let that go. I was destined to do great things and heal many people. He spoke of my youth and sent me lots of love. It was absolutely beautiful to hear for my granddad in this way, years and years after his passing. That was it for night one, I met Mike in the hallway and it was time for dinner so we went into the dining hall. It was buffet style and the choice was great for us vegetarians, which was a surprise because that is not usually the case. We had been told in the meeting earlier that day, that whatever table we sat at tonight we were to sit there for every meal, just incase of emergency so we could be found quickly. The room was quiet full and a lot of tables were already taken. I spotted a table up the top of the room with some ladies at it and a few empty seats so I pointed to Mike to follow me. When we got to the table there was two seats left so the ladies warmly welcomed us and we all introduced ourselves.

One of the ladies was in my group and one of them was in Mike's group and the other two ladies were in the same group, which was different to ours. The conversation at dinner was awesome. We spoke of our tutors and our first experiences in class. We were all very excited about our groups and tutors. I knew then I was in the right group, there are no mistakes! That night we were both very tired after our eventful evening and went to our room and did a relaxing meditation. We had a cup of tea and discussed our group activity and the schedule as we knew it for tomorrow. I could not sleep at all that night. The place was filled with spirit activity and they kept coming to me. At five am I got fed up of being awake so I did a deep grounding meditation and asked Archangel Michael to keep any spirits away from me for the rest of the night. That worked a treat and I slept sound until the alarm went off less than three hours later! As always I was so grateful to Archangel Michael.

We took a walk before going to breakfast and then made our way to class. We all took pretty much the same seats we had sat on last night and this time Patricia said she wanted us to say a little about ourselves and what we wanted help with. This time she started at the other side of the room so I was almost last up before break time. I was feeling a bit nervous as I had not spoken to a group that size in a long time.

When it was my turn I said "I'm Jane and I am from Ireland. I have never sat in circle before". Patricia then said "did you grow up in a haunted house?" I said "no, not that I know of ".Then Patricia said "I can see you at the age of about four and there are a lot of spirit children around you. Jane you have seen and felt a lot of spirit "Yes Patricia I have" I replied." Are you interested in E.V.P?" Patricia asked me. I replied "I don't know what that is ". Patricia replied "It's the paranormal and supernatural; I see a lot of that activity around you". I replied" I am very interested in it alright but I don't know much at all about it". Patricia then said "there is a broken down church near to where you live, there is a job for you to do there if you wish to do it. When you think of the place email it to me and I will tell you then." I replied Thank you Patricia. I did not meet up with Mike at break time; he went for a healing instead so we did not catch up until lunchtime.

Mike was feeling great and very excited about the progress he was making with his tutor. I filled him in on my morning and the readings I had done before lunch, we had paired off every twenty minutes to make connections to spirit and bring messages through for each other. I had received and given some wonderful messages from loved ones in spirit from and to the other mediums I had paired up with. We were able to go for a walk and have a lovely chat about everything before we went back to class. It was a beautiful spring like day and we were feeling blessed. My evening was very intensive and a lot of mental medium ship which can be very tiring. I was exhausted by dinner time. I met Mike and the other ladies in the dining room and we ate in semi silence.

We were all wiped out! Mike and I went for a lie down before the public demonstrations that night. It was a fabulous night. Every one who spoke was very professional. I marveled at their nerves to stand up and do that in a full hall, I didn't think I could ever be confident enough to do that. After that, we were free to do as we wished. Some people went to the bar, some went to town and some like me and Mike went to bed. We did a beautiful laying down meditation to relax our minds after the taxing day. It was such a treat to relax and unwind. I went for a shower to refresh my tired body and felt semi normal after that, Mike napped while I showered .Then I made us both a cup of green tea before we went to sleep for the night. We both slept sound thankfully on our second night there. We woke feeling refreshed and raring to go on Sunday morning.

The weekend was flying and we would be going home this evening. After breakfast we went straight to class. We did some medium ship connections for each other, moving all around the room. Bringing through two or more family members from spirit to the person we were reading for, It was awesome! I loved every single minute of it. I met Mike at break and he was very excited with his morning and what had occurred. We would be finished our course the next time we would meet at lunch! When we went back Patricia took the time to work her way around the room and give us her report on us, what we would be good at, or what other types of medium ship we could explore, things like that. It was amazing the amount of us that had confidence issues! When it came to my turn Patricia said "Jane you will make a wonderful teacher or lecturer and your very sensitive nature makes for wonderful private readings. Platform work is also strongly there for you, you should pursue it. Paranormal is something you may wish to develop, it's entirely up to you, but it is for you if want to work in that area, you will be very good at it. Now Jane I want you to promise me that you won't just go home and do nothing after this." I smiled and gave a nervous laugh; I knew I had been guilty of procrastinating for far too long. "Spirit is telling me that you should have been doing this for three years. Spirit has no voice without you Jane, it is something you must do with the gifts and talents you have. Your dad is here with me now and he is delighted that your confidence is back, now when he says back that means it has been gone but you did have it before". I nodded in agreement." He is very emotional and full of love for you". Patricia said. I thanked her for her input and kind words. I felt excited at the thoughts of going back home and working as a medium, I knew at some level, that this is what I was there to do. I noticed that Patricia never said about the paranormal and supernatural work, to any of the other mediums in the room, interesting I thought, very very interesting. Especially with all the supernatural things that had occurred in my life lately!

It was almost time to say goodbye to all at the College when I met up with Mike for lunch. I was telling him all about the tools for practice I had learned, some business and legal tips too. Mike filled me in on his practice work he was bringing home with him. We were both thrilled and delighted. After lunch we went for a walk around the grounds and made our way over to the graveyard and the tombs.

I had read a little about the founder of the college, before we came, he was an extra ordinary man. I thanked him for The College and what I had learnt here. I felt I could not have got so much from a course any where else in the world. I took some photographs and there was a beautiful white orb near his tomb and I knew that he was with us and appreciating our visit. I exchanged numbers with some of the ladies on the course before saying goodbye. We shared a taxi to the airport with a German lady who had been sitting with us at meal times from the first meal. Her flight was an hour before ours so we waited with her until it was time to say goodbye. Mike and I had so much to talk about on the plane trip home; you would think we had not seen each other all weekend! It was great to be home too, the children were all excited to see they had got on beautifully without us! After lots of hugs and kisses later we gave them some gifts we had picked for them at the airport. The next morning I took on board what Patricia my tutor had said to me and I stepped up as a spirit medium to the world. It was scary, but exciting!

I posted on my healing page on face book and my personal page that I had just returned from the college and now could add medium ship services to my list of services I offered. The response was fantastic I was overwhelmed by the congratulations, well wishes, shares, messages and booking I received. I was not expecting that huge response and I felt so blessed to receive such support as I stepped into being me. I created an event for Friday for a day of medium ship sittings now that I had my confidence back. Wahoo bring it on, I could not wait! I received bookings for two healings and three medium readings for that Friday. That was more than enough for one day I was over the moon.

My clients were such beautiful people and their loved ones in spirit were simply amazing .The depth of detail they gave to me to pass on to each client was phenomenal. Each session had stories, tears, laughter and memories of times together. They were absolutely beautiful healing experiences. I was so happy, overjoyed and tired at the end of the day. I needed to work these new muscles I was using to connect with spirit for my clients, I was exhausted from the three today! I sat in gratitude to thank God for the blessings overflowing in my life; my heart was bursting with thanks. I went to bed early that night and slept sound until morning. I woke early in the morning and did my usual prayer and meditation routine. I was going through yesterday in my head and could not stop smiling. I thought of what my tutor had told me in the college and decided to check out doing a public demonstration in Killarney in the near future. Life is so awesome when we get out of our own way!

CHAPTER 6

Being a Medium

Later the next morning I went online and looked for prices on event rooms in local hotels in Killarney. By lunch time I had replies and decided on one in particular. I rang the number and spoke to the lady in charge of events .We agreed to meet the next day at 2 o clock, for me to view the room. Mike covered the shop while I walked up to the hotel. As I walked up I wondered when my life had become so blessed. Everything I could ever have dreamed of and more was now in my life. As I entered the hotel I saw the reception desk off to my left. I went over and asked for the events lady. After a few moments she appeared and walked me to the room. It was a big room and it was beautiful. Oh my God I thought, this will be awesome for a night of medium ship. I loved it .It could seat on hundred people.

I booked it there and then for Friday the 11ᵗʰ of March at 7.30pm. Well that was easy I thought, as I walked back to the shop, or maybe I skipped back! I was over the moon with happiness. There would be no stopping me now! The next day I had a client booked in for a healing, before some angel card readings and the rest of the day I spent in the shop. My client for healing presented herself with crying all the time and she did not know why. When Gillian lay on the therapy bed I could see a lady holding a very tiny baby standing to the right of us.

I welcomed the two of them, the spirit visitors and I began the healing session. All of her chakras were unbalanced and her heart chakra was the worst. There was a lot of energy releasing in this session.

Afterwards as she sat on the edge of the bed describing how light and good she felt. I gently asked her if she had lost someone very close to her recently as I felt her unprocessed grief was a lot to do with her crying. She began to sob as she said her mother had died ten months ago, and she herself had a miscarriage with her baby two months ago. She went on to say she was so mad at her mother for not being there for her, when she needed her most in her life. I walked to her and wrapped my arms around her, she melted into me and cried and cried for the longest time. Deep heart wrenching tears of sadness, anger, grief and pain. She said she could never forgive her mother for leaving her; she should have stayed with her as they had always a very close relationship. I prayed for Gillian as she held onto me, Please God Help her. When she had calmed down and the tears stopped I told her who I had seen and that they both had come to say hello and give you support today. I explained how her baby was with her mother in the spirit world, and her mother was looking after him now. She said that she would want no one better to care for her child than her mother, when she herself could not do it. I said if your mother were not in spirit she could not do this for you. She looked at me when I said this to her and I saw a change in her eyes as she took this statement to heart. She then said "I have hated my mother for two months and feeling so lost and abandoned have been looking at this all wrong". She began to cry again as she apologized to her mother and thanked her for looking after her little angel. It was an extremely emotional experience for both of us; my heart went out to this beautiful lady. I thanked God for the healing she had received today and I knew in my heart and soul it would change the rest of her life. She was in a much more peaceful place when she left me that day. I could not get her out of mind all day so I lit a candle for her mom, herself and her baby. We never know what hardships other people have; my client had been in deep crisis, God Bless her. She returned two weeks later with a bounce in her step. I told her she looked amazing .She thanked me and thanked me for all I had done for her, she would be eternally grateful. She thanked me for helping her, her relationship with her husband was better than it ever had been. I thanked God for what he had done for this beautiful young woman and all those around her. Now she had her peace of mind back she realized how precious it was. Gillian told me she had started a new job and she was thrilled with the new improved relationship with her husband. She told me I had helped her beyond words because she could not forgive her mother before and the hatred had been eating her inside.

On the 12th of February I held my first full medium ship day in Donnelly's Shop. Mike worked the shop whilst I saw clients in my little angel room behind the counter. I was a nervous wreck; all those old doubts came creeping back in. I seriously needed to have words with myself; I was not going back down the road to no confidence. I sat in meditation for along time to quite my mind. After that I felt excited and I was so looking forward to the day with spirit. I felt honored and humbled at the same time to be a true voice of spirit to people who were missing their loved ones.

As always my clients that day were all such lovely people. There was plenty laughter and some tears too. A really beautiful day was had by us all. I felt such a well of gratitude for this day that was filled with so many blessings not only for me but for all my clients and those they could share their story within I thanked God for this wonderful and special gift he gave to me; to be a bridge between those grieving their loved ones, to their loved ones in spirit. The next day I had some clients in an teach for healings. My last client of the day presented with chronic back pain and had been unable to work or even able to walk very far in the past three weeks. She had seen a sticker on the side of my car and that is how she found me! As I laid my hands on her head the room filled with the most vibrant purple. I always call upon Archangel Michael for all healings to do some gentle chord cutting and I just knew this was him! Oh my God it was fantastic and the energy in the room was magnificent .I knew this client would receive a huge healing. The healing session went beautifully. My client had become very relaxed and even fell asleep for a lot of it! When she came around after I had finished she said that she had never felt as relaxed in her entire life as she just had. She then sat up with no mobility issue and said she was not sure if she still had pain. She was in pain for so long she was afraid to say it was gone. She also had seen the purple through her closed eyes and asked "was that an angel? It just felt so beautiful I thought it might be an angel." I then told her about Archangel Michael and she was amazed! I told her to increase her water intake to help the energies shift some more to enable a deeper healing experience. She walked to her car with a little limp but good mobility otherwise.

I have always had the will and desire to help others, now I was feeling such gratitude for my days helping others. I now also help them to heal on many different levels which are all just awesome. Once I had the room cleaned down and saged, I knelt down in prayer to Thank God for all he did for me. Also to tell him how humbled I was to be his servant and to do Our Lord's Work every day. The next day was Sunday, and Sunday is our family day. We all look forward to this special time alone as a family to connect with each other and have fun. We never accept individual invitations to anywhere on a Sunday, it's an unspoken rule that we all very much agree on. This day we decided to go for a drive through the Gap of Dunloe. It was a beautiful day, for this most scenic of drives. The sky was blue and there was hardly a cloud to be seen. This is unusual weather for February in Ireland so we were making the most of it. I took lots of photos as we drove through; it is such a beautiful place in this world. We drove on then to Kenmare and had lunch in a lovely restaurant before driving home. When we looked at the photographs later they were spectacular! We could not count the amount of angel orbs we saw in them! We had such a beautiful day together which was full of fun with beautiful memories made and now these angel orbs to finish off a perfect day. The next few weeks I was busy working the shop by day and seeing clients in the evenings for healings and readings.

March 11th rolled round so fast I didn't have much time to get nervous. I was really looking forward to it, there was a great buzz about town about it and all tickets had almost sold out. I had limited the event to 50 people, as I did not feel I would cope with talking in front of a larger group. That old confidence thing again! That morning I was fine when I got up but as the day moved on I began to feel sick with nerves. I was going to be doing my first public demonstration of medium ship .Was I gone mad? Had I completely lost my mind? Well it was too late to back out now I told myself! Mike came in to me at lunch time and told me to take some time in meditation, to help calm my emotions, so I didn't say no! I went into my little angel reading room and sat in meditation for half an hour. I felt amazing afterwards having connected with my guide Jane and she had assured me it would be an amazing evening and that I would shine.

I closed the shop at 6pm and Mike brought in my suitcase with some make up and a change of clothes that I personally had needed. It also contained a salt lamp, an angel, some candles and incense for my table at the event. I got changed quickly and we made our way to the hotel. I wanted to be there early to clear and sage the room to increase the energy in it, to make it more conductive to spirit. I then sat in meditation and actively worked on connecting with spirit for the night. Then I was all set. People soon began to fill the room. I knew some of the people but most of them I had never seen before. I sat in gratitude as they all sat down; all of these people have put their trust and faith in me, that I can do what I say I will. I felt deeply humbled by this. I felt so grateful that they were putting their faith and hope in me. Fifty one people sat before me, waiting for the night to begin. I said a quick prayer before I stood up to speak "dear Lord please help me to heal everyone in this room tonight, Amen". I walked to the centre of the top of the room. I introduced myself and spoke a little about myself. My voice began to shake and I was feeling nervous so I cut short my prepared introduction speech. I then asked the audience to close their eyes and to take in a few slow deep breaths. This would relax any fears or nerves they may have had and also raise the energy in the room. I also closed my eyes and took in three deep breaths as I invited a member of the spirit world to come join me.

On the third breath out I felt a male spirit join me. I welcomed the spirit and thanked him for coming first and so quickly. I then proceeded to pass on any information this man gave to me for his family member in the audience. There were a lot of spirit connections that night and it was so beautiful. As soon as spirit connected with me my nerves disappeared. I was calm and centered, as I focused on the information that was coming to me in thought, feeling and picture. Everyone in the audience recognized their family member, with the information I was relaying from spirit. It was really beautiful. As I finished up, I thanked everyone for coming and for being so nice to me, I truly appreciated it. The reaction from the crowd was powerful and overwhelming. Everyone came up to shake my hand or hug me and to thank me and congratulate me on a wonderful night. When I had tidied up and put my things back in the case, I took a moment to thank all the spirits who came through tonight, to thank my guide Jane who is awesome to me, to thank Jesus and Mary and God. I said thank you for the successful evening as it was off the charts on the scale of a success. I was very thirsty when I got home and drank a pint of water, then another one before I could sit and relax for the night. My heart was filled with so much love and happiness I drifted into a deep and peaceful sleep.

The next morning I woke up feeling very tired. I really needed to hydrate my body after last night; it had taken a lot out of me. I spent a lot of the day sitting in the shop, relaxing as much as I could until my energy levels picked up again. All day people were coming in to congratulate me and those who received messages were so grateful. The rest of the month went by in a blur of medium readings, angel readings, healings, shop work and family time! My medium connections were getting much stronger with all the work I was now doing, it was awesome.

Around this time I noticed a deepening in my healings as well .The feedback from clients was so positive, I was humbled by it. Life is so amazing! I felt so grateful for the connection with spirit and the angels and to God every day now and I was sure feeling the blessings of this too. Every night I sat in meditation in candlelight, a beautiful orb had started to fly around the room, each night. It was so beautiful to watch and the energy of pure love that radiated from the orb, it was magnificent! I knew it was my dad and that made my heart sing with utter joy. He passed away in 1999 and there was not a day I did not miss his physical presence in my life. We have a very special relationship and for that I am extremely grateful! On Friday night April 1st. I went to bed around 11pm. I had a very fitful sleep. There was a lot of spirit activity in my bedroom. The best way I can describe it is; it was like I was in a waiting room at a train station and crowds of people were filing in and out, talking and rushing by. The energy was loud and chaotic. I heard someone say "these are lost souls".

The next morning I woke up very tired and instantly remembered what had happened last night. I was trying to make sense of it in my head. I had no idea what realm I had been in because the lost souls did not appear to be in mine, I seemed to be in there's! I felt it in my bones that some big changes were on the way. The butterflies in my stomach began to flutter and grow. Exciting times ahead, I knew it! The next night I went to bed at 10.30pm because I was really tired from last nights adventure. I woke up at 4am and could not go back to sleep. I tossed and turned for a while, but there was to be no more sleep for me. I got up and went to sit in the sitting room, and tucked myself under a fluffy throw. I decided to meditate; I felt I would receive guidance, as I believed the angels had woken me to give me a message. I became very relaxed very quickly and went into a deep meditation. I received guidance that I was to write a book and also to set up and teach a guardian angel course. I took this advice on board and it resonated strongly within me. I needed to become better known so that I could help more people, this was the message.

I put the book on the back burner' and focused on creating a course for The Guardian angel day. In the past few years I had learnt so much on the angels, and from the Angels. I had begun to see the Angels, work with the Angels and receive guidance from the Angels. I love the Angels and I am so grateful for their presence in my life, filling it with blessings each and every moment of each and every day. It was fun and easy for me to get my course work together and in order for the day. All those books and the courses I had read and taken stood to me now. It didn't go unnoticed by me either that quiet recently I had re read all my books on angels so everything was fresh in my mind. I laughed at the thought of this, because God and the angels are always steps way ahead of us! I was following the guidance I was being given and everything flowed smoothly. I was feeling so excited to be bringing the angels into peoples lives, to fill their lives with blessings. I knew what this could do for them, as I knew first hand what the Angels had done for me and my family. It was awesome.

I felt very strongly that everyone should be aware that each of us has a guardian angel assigned to us at birth. As we have free will given to us by God, the Angels need to be asked by us to assist us with our day to day worries or tasks. When we bring the angels into our lives, the blessings are tremendous and life becomes blessed. My healing page on face book was really gaining momentum now. The likes, comments and shares were amazing. I was extremely grateful to all these lovely people who were open to learning and growing spiritually with me on Jane's energy healing page. I was receiving a lot of private messages and was able to help people in a private way with any worries or queries they had regarding sickness or spirit activity, or anything slightly related to all of this.

I received a booking from a lady in London over the internet. She believed there was a spirit in her home and that her house was haunted. She told me of some instance's which had occurred and I began to think she was correct in her thinking. She sent me on what I needed, to be able to tune into her home. At 8 pm that night I set up my little alter and lit some candles .I tuned into her home and instantly felt the presence of spirit. It was a male and he was aged fifty I felt. I began my routine which I had now developed for sending souls to the light and I sent this soul to Heaven. I then energetically cleaned her entire home and asked the angels to protect her and her home. I sent a text her to tell her I was finished and told her that I would ring her in the morning to fill her in.

The next morning, first thing I rang her. She was so excited; she had the best nights sleep in years! She could not describe how light and clean her home felt, it was as if everything now shone inside there. I told her about the male presence in her home and that he was now no longer there. I then explained how the energy changed for the better in her home because of this. She said she knew it was a strange thing to say but she felt that her home was now her own. She had lived there for four years with this spirit. Now he was gone she could feel it. I was so happy for her, she was such a kindhearted lady and she deserved peace in her own home. I felt vey thankful that I was involved in bringing this peace to her. The rest of the day I was busy putting the final touches to my Guardian Angel workshop that was happening the next day. There were five people booked in for it and I was super excited.

Saturday April 9ᵗʰ was the angel workshop day. I woke up before the alarm went off and I was full of joy, today would be an amazing day, blessings and miracles! I placed the sheets and the handouts on the table, all ready for my students. They were jammed pack with information on Angels, Guardian Angels, Archangels, and all things angelic. I received one cancellation text from a lady Nora from North Limerick, she was called in to work and had no choice but to go in. I told her this was ok and maybe next time she would make the workshop, I would let her know when it was on. I strongly believed that whoever was meant to be would be here. Everything happens for a reason. I was collecting three people in town, one from the train and two from the bus. The others were making their own way to my house. I drove in to the train station and met a lady named Charlotte. We sat in my car and chatted whilst waiting for the man and woman from Tipperary to arrive on the bus .We discovered whilst talking that we both each have one daughter and both our little ladies share the same birthday date, are the same age and were born on the same day in the same hospital! How mad was that? When the two arrived it was two ladies, not a man and a woman as booked. The man had opted out and his wife came down instead. So it was I and all these lovely ladies for the Guardian Angel day, just as it was supposed to be.

The ladies were all sensitive, caring, giving and loving individuals. They loved the angel meditations we did. They soaked up all the information on angels and had any questions they had answered. We had a lovely salad for lunch and then went for a short walk outside to stretch our legs. It was a beautiful day, blue skies and sunshine. After lunch the ladies sat for a meditation, they closed their eyes and I began to read out an angel meditation I had written specially for today. I saw three beautifully white orbs flying between and around their heads, as they meditated. My heart was overflowing with love and blessings. The day went very quickly and we were a little sad when it was all over. We all had an amazingly beautiful day. Each of us had felt the angel energy in the room. All of the ladies had connected with their Guardian angel and now knew their guardian angels names. I knew that this was the beginning of very important changes for each of these ladies and that this was only the beginning! I sat in meditation for a long time that night and gave thanks for all the love, support and guidance I receive from the angels. Today would never have happened without my angel's guidance. I made some new and wonderful friends that day and that was divinely planned with Divine timing. I also thanked the angels that I had the ability to receive and acknowledge all their angelic help.

The next day was Sunday and I felt very tired. Working with the angels yesterday had taken a lot of energy from me. We went for a leisurely walk and had a very relaxed family day. We ate lunch in town so that meant no cooking for me. That evening Mike was practicing his medium ship work. I was teaching him techniques and encouraging him with developing his skills. He made a wonderful breakthrough and connected with spirit. He was thrilled beyond words to have done this. I was absolutely delighted for him. He had been working on and off on this since we returned from the College. When I sat in meditation it came to me that I was now officially a teacher! That was simply amazing, how did that happen so quickly and without my full awareness? Pure awesomeness is what it was!

The next morning I received a phone call from a man called Pat in Derry. He was in a slightly distressed state. He had seen a shadow man in his home last night. I reassured him that everything would be alright and there was nothing to fear. He gave me what information I needed so I scheduled the spirit removal and house clearing for that evening, when I would be available to do it. At 9 pm I energetically tuned in to Pat's home and I instantly felt nauseous. I called on Archangel Michael to protect me as I did this work. There were two spirit entities there in his home. One went to the light easily and the other shadowy one put up a little struggle but went to the light in the end. The sick feeling in my stomach left me then. I finished off by clearing and blessing the house. I felt extremely drained after this job. I began to recognize that working with different energies, either higher or lower vibrations demanded more energy from me. I was fascinated by this; I found it to be very interesting. Pat had pretty much the same feedback as the first house clearing I had done. The one big difference was that he had nausea and headaches for the six months since he had moved into that house and this morning he was well. I told him of the nausea I experienced when I tuned into his home. I also explained to him that it had left me, when the shadow man he had seen moved into the light. He was extremely grateful to me and quiet emotional about it too. I thanked him for trusting me to help him and wished him health and happiness in his new home.

The next evening we had just finished our dinner and as we do when the children get up and leave the table, Mike and I sit to talk about our day. We were happily chatting away when out of the corner of my eye; I saw a huge bright white light. I turned my head as I caught sight of the biggest brightest whitest light fly past the window. It was an Angel! Oh My God, my heart filled with a huge swell of love and peace. It was spectacular! "Mike said what you are looking at"? I could not reply for a minute, I was enraptured. When the angel left I returned my attention to Mike. Mike had been at a different angle to the window that I, so he had not seen it. I explained as good as I could, as to what I had just seen and felt, but I really could not put words to the emotions in my heart and soul. I was in a state of bliss for the rest of the evening.

The next morning I woke up early, an hour before the alarm would go off and I then decided I would get up and I would go outside to pray today. It was a beautiful warm morning, with the sun shining high in the sky so early in the day. All was well in my world and I really wanted to give thanks for that. I then went into (an teach) my healing house and meditated for twenty minutes before going into the house, to get ready for my days work in the shop. On my way to work I met a lady I knew called Frances on the main street, she appeared to be in a very distressed state. She seemed to be in a panic or some kind of crisis. I told her to take a deep breath and I assured her everything would be ok. I told her to take her time. After a little while she began to talk, she told me that strange things had been happening in her house. Keys were being moved, cupboards opening, pictures falling off walls and a host of other activities. Frances went on to tell me she had gone for a bath last night and when she opened the bathroom door to leave, there was a big shadow man with a hat standing right in front of her. She got the fright of her life and stepped back into the bathroom in terror. She stayed in there for a while before shouting to her husband to come upstairs. When her husband arrived on the landing he asked her what she wanted, she asked him "can you see anyone out there with you?" Her husband was puzzled at this question, as there was only the two of them in the house all evening. He replied "it's only me here". The lady then came out of her bathroom and told her husband what she had seen.

A friend of his had heard about me and decided it was necessary to meet me. She had been unable to sleep a wink last night as she was petrified that, that thing would come near her. I spoke with her and reassured her that I could indeed help her. I scheduled this job, to do the spirit removal and house clearance just after 6 pm when the shop closed. She wanted me to go to her home as she was too afraid the remote removal would not work. It was not too far so to allay her fears, I was at her home twenty minutes later. As soon as I set foot inside the door of her house, I could feel his presence. I could also sense he was hiding. I set up my little alter with some sage, a candle and an Archangel Michael Statue. I quieted my mind and tuned in to the angels, I sent that spirit to the light and the energy in the house shifted hugely. The lights flickered and I knew he was now where he was supposed to be and not in this house anymore. I then went and opened all the windows and lit some white sage.

I smudged the place from bottom to top and by the time I finished the fresh air flowing through the house was very refreshing. That poor lady looked so much better than she had this morning. I knew that they would both sleep soundly tonight, both she and her husband. I was so happy that I could help them both and to have the problem removed in such a quick time for her and her family. Also that the soul was sent back to God. Frances and her husband Joe were lovely people and were so grateful to me for what I had just done. Their children were at their grandmothers for the evening until I finished the clearing so I hadn't met them. They asked me some questions relating to the strange activity in their home and I assured them that all those issues had now been dealt with and their home would be fine now. As I sat into my car to go home I thanked God for this gift he gave to me to help these people, to help the trapped spirit and to do God's work at the same time. Amen.

The next day was Saturday and it was a beautiful sunny morning. I was driving in to the shop, when the most amazingly bright white huge circle of light came from my left, flew slowly past my windscreen and continued off to my right and then vanished! I smiled; I knew this was an angel, I could feel it! Oh wow. Oh wow. How awesome was that? My heart was overflowing with love and peace, joy and happiness. It was going to be another blessed and amazing day, "Thank you angels as always" I said. The following Tuesday I was only in the shop until one o clock and then I was home with the children for the rest of the day, once they finished school. I opened all the windows and decided to give the house a good airing and a spring clean, it was a warm sunny day outside and the children played happily out there. I had a client booked for a healing at 8pm so I had plenty of time to do all that I wanted before that time. I even got ten minutes to sit in the sun, as I watched the children jump on the trampoline, my life felt perfect and I loved every single moment of it. I was cooking a vegetarian goulash for the first time for dinner so that took me a bit longer to prepare than it should have. The smells from the kitchen were delicious whilst the goulash was simmering and the potatoes were steaming. Mike arrived home just in time and everyone was hungry after all the fresh air of the day. We ate our dinner at 7pm and it was so tasty, we all agreed I should cook it again real soon. I had the healing house all ready for my client at 8pm so I was able relax at the dining table after we had eaten and chat with Mike as usual.

At quarter to eight I went out and turned on the heater to give the room a cozy feel and a warm glow. I then lit some candles and did a mini meditation to centre and ground myself in preparation for my client. I returned into the house and Mike said my phone had received a message, so I went to check it. At three minutes to eight my client text to cancel the healing session. I felt slightly annoyed that she had not let me know earlier, it really was such short notice. Not to worry I thought, everything happens for a reason. There must be a valid reason, so I sent her a text saying that was ok, and I said a quick prayer for her. I then went out to the healing room and blew out the candles and turned off the heater. It was almost ready for the next client I thought as I shut the door behind me. I informed Mike of the cancellation when I saw him again, he suggested as I was now free for the night we could go for a walk in the national park. I thought this was a great idea and so did Hannah and Michael.

We quickly got ready and drove the six or seven minutes to the national park. It was a glorious evening, as we walked by the lake shore. I happily snapped some photos as we walked, or I got Mike and the children to stand in for a scenic shot here and there. We walked for miles; it was the most we had walked in a very long time! as Michael did not like to walk. Tonight he seemed to have forgotten that! The energy around us was amazing, the sun shone so brightly reflecting off the water, we all felt in holiday mode! I could see some beautiful orbs flying around as we walked and totally felt their blessings. We sat for a while and watched the sunset and then we went home. The photographs were spectacular, the vibrancy and varied colours of the orbs were magnificent! Archangel coloured orbs, angel white orbs and green orbs with tiny dots inside fairy orbs. No wonder we had all felt so energized to walk that long!

Once the children went to bed Mike and I sat in meditation, we listened to a powerful guided Archangel Michael meditation. It was such a beautiful experience. Mike practiced his medium work and connected to my dad and gave me a short message. I was delighted, so happy to hear from my dad, and so happy for Mike to connect with spirit this way. Mike could not maintain the connection for very long and that was just fine. He was only learning and I had been the same when I was just beginning too. Mike was a bit disheartened it didn't last longer for my sake. I assured him he had done really well and to focus on the good parts only, he should be proud, he had made great progress tonight. Mike went to the kitchen to get us both a drink of water and then I heard him call me to join him there.

In our home the kitchen and dining are more or less one big room, but the dividing wall, which was to be arched and as yet has not been, has pictures of our loved ones in spirit on the kitchen side of that wall and pictures of us through the years on the dining room side of the wall. Mike told me that while he was filling the glass with water, from the big bottle of water from the fridge, something brought his attention to my dad's picture up on the wall. He then asked me to look at the picture and tell him what I was seeing. I looked at the picture of my dad and I could not believe my eyes, but I knew Mike must be seeing the same, otherwise why had he called me out to look at this? I replied "I see my dad, then I see his face disappearing and other faces going where his face should be"." That's exactly what I saw when I turned my attention to the photograph and called you out" Mike said. We both stood there with our mouths open watching face after face sit on my dad neck in his photograph .This was absolutely mind-blowing. I went and got my phone and hoped these phenomena could be captured on camera. When I returned to the kitchen it was still happening so I made a little video and then took some photos. It was incredible to watch, unbelievable really! "This is a message from my dad for you, and it is to help you with your medium ship" I said to Mike. Mike replied, "Ah, I get it now, I know exactly what this means"! We stayed watching the faces change on the photograph for another half an hour before eventually going to bed .It was truly spectacular and we were mesmerized by it .We both felt so blessed by this magical spiritual experience.

Monday April 20th was Mike's last day of Chemotherapy treatment, six of six! I got up earlier than usual that morning because I wanted to cook Mike some breakfast as he would have no appetite for a few days after the chemotherapy. He was in great form when he woke up and delighted to smell the lovely breakfast I had cooked for him. We chatted about the day ahead as he ate and Mike was feeling very excited and positive. When it was time for Mike to head to the hospital I gave him a long hug and an even longer kiss goodbye. I called on Archangel Michael to go with Mike to protect him and I called on other angels too to ease his day. As I waved Mike off I prayed to God, to please let Mike be healed. The results would not be in until after the scan next week so it would be about two weeks time when we would know. It was a matter of faith and trust.

CHAPTER 7

Carrying On

The following Friday I began an online fairyology course. I was so excited, I had recently started to see tree spirits and I really wanted to learn all I could about trees and the fairy realms that I was now tuning into. The course did not disappoint me. On Sunday we went for a beautiful walk by the river. It was really the most gorgeous of days. I could see so many spirit faces in the trees, it was phenomenal! We walked to the lake shore and collected some stones there. I wanted to create a fairy ring in our garden once we got home. I had learnt about it in the course the day before and I was feeling super excited at this new project.

Hannah was mega excited too, skipping, singing and jumping at the thoughts of seeing the fairies real soon! We had a little picnic at the lakeshore of salad rolls, fruit and crisps, washed down with some flavored water. We then began walking back along the river path to the car. Once home we all went out into the garden near the bird feeder and picked a place for the fairy ring. Mike placed the stones and Hannah and I placed a little fairy house and some shiny pebbles inside the circle. It looked awesome! I took some photographs and we were rewarded with a beautiful orb and with a lot of fairy activity too. I made a short video because the energy was so totally incredible. It was absolutely amazing to watch the orb fly around our little fairy ring. I went to bed at around eleven pm that night and was woken at 4.44am. In angel numbers 444 means you are surrounded by loving angels being guided and supported. I love getting messages from the angels in this way and it happens so often now that I truly value the guidance and support I receive. I woke when the alarm went off the next morning and jumped right out of bed. I felt excited and energized. I could feel changes in the air!

It was a beautiful sunny morning so I decided to take the scenic route to work, a little walk in nature before opening the shop. I felt so connected to it all and so very blessed. I had some clients for medium ship and each one was a lovely healing experience. That night I went to bed at ten thirty pm and slept sound until I was woken at 5.55am. I knew that number 5 in angel numbers signifies change so I happily dozed back to sleep until 6.35am. When I got up I checked my angel numbers, as the kettle was boiling. I read that 555 is a triple number so it is strongly emphasized. It meant big change was coming up for me and to prepare for it now. These changes were divinely inspired and guided. These changes would fully align me with my true Divine Purpose and my soul mission. Wow, I felt so excited I could hardly breathe. I had felt this big change for a while now in the air and now the angels were confirming it. Oh my God what was going to happen? The next morning I took the scenic walk again and soaked in the beauty of the day and my surroundings. Nature is so beautiful, the weather was stunning and I was feeling the blessings in my life, deep within my heart and soul. Days like these are heavenly.

The following Friday I had an outside call to do for a lady who was temporarily housebound. I do not usually do house calls, for personal safety reasons, but I knew the area this lady lived and as it was a nursing home I felt safe enough to go there. She was experiencing severe swelling in both of her legs, from her knees down to her toes. Her legs were rock hard to touch and appeared to be in a lot of pain. We spoke for a little while and Noreen told me she had been unable to walk for days. As soon as I placed my hands on her head she fell asleep, almost instantly. A few minutes into her healing session I got pains in my legs, the pain became excruciating and I thought I would have to sit down. I was shuffling from foot to foot to alleviate the pains.

Noreen was sitting on a reclining chair with her feet up on a footstool. I decided to kneel on the carpeted floor as I worked on her legs', the pain was still very bad, I was getting no relief like this, so I tried sitting on the carpet then. This pain in my legs was crippling me. I stood up again as I moved down to her feet. The heat transmitting from the soles of her feet was so intense. The energy release was just huge. With that burst of energy from the bottom of her feet, the pain in my legs disappeared. In that instant I knew that pain had been Noreen's and not mine. How did that happen? How did her pain travel through me? I had felt the pain in her body, travel through my body then release. I knew she was no longer in any pain as when it had left me it also left her!

This was incredible! I was so happy for her because she had suffered greatly with that horrible pain and now it was gone! I knew this for sure as I too had suffered with it for a short time. When I finished the healing session I gently woke Noreen. She said she felt great and her legs felt a lot better already. She could hardly believe it when I described her pain to her and where the most painful parts of her legs were. I told her that her pain had travelled through me before releasing. She thanked me and told me I had the gift and also the most gentlest of touches with my hands. Noreen was walking later that evening and the next day she was out and about in the gardens .Thank you God for the gifts you bestow on me and thank you for helping me to heal Noreen.

The following Tuesday Mike was back to meet with the specialist, the results were in form the last Chemotherapy round. Mike was feeling excited and a little anxious as to what today's news would be. Health wise he was feeling a lot fitter and stronger so his body was telling him that he was improving. The lumps in his lungs had shrunk but no movement on the cancer in his bones. We had mixed emotions at his news but quickly focused on the positive, the lumps had shrunk, to us that meant they were no longer cancerous! Cancer cells keep growing and multiplying, they do not shrink. The specialist suggested to Mike that he continue on a maintenance dose of Chemotherapy to keep things as they were now. Mike agreed and would begin his maintenance chemotherapy the following week. Mikes body did not respond well to this new form of chemotherapy, he was very unwell almost as soon as he returned home from the hospital that day. He was extremely cold, highly nauseous, had severe pains in his limbs, pins and needles in his feet and numbness in his toes. I tucked him up on the recliner couch and turned on the oil heating, to heat the house quickly. Mike fell asleep almost instantly and I thanked God for that as he desperately needed some relief.

That evening I gave him a healing and he felt a lot better, he went to bed and slept soundly. It occurred to me that Mike was healthier and stronger in the last two weeks with no chemotherapy than now, did that mean he no longer needed it? My head was filled with scenarios, miracle healings, prayers, faith, and trust in God as I finally drifted off to sleep. I asked the angels for guidance so that I could help my husband.

Monday 2ⁿᵈ May was a bank holiday in Ireland so we were all home this day. A day off work and school! I heated my little healing house and put some frankincense oil on the burner, as I prepared the room to treat Mike to a bonus healing session. I gathered some crystals, I was going to use on Mike to magnify the healing that was going to take place. An hour later I told Mike I had an teach ready for him, all he had to do was go out there and lie down. Mike was delighted and out we both went. He lay on the bed and I covered him with a warm blanket. I then placed some crystals on and near him. As soon as I joined my hands in prayer at the top of the therapy bed I could feel the energy in the air, it was electric. I could sense spirit also in the room with us and I silently welcomed them. I laid my hands on Mike and began the healing; the release of energy was powerful, as I worked my way down Mike's body all the way to his feet. When I put my hands on Mike's feet, his mother Hannah Mai appeared next to me, I smiled and silently said hello to her. She smiled back at me and asked me if she could work through me and touch Mike's toes. I said absolutely Hannah you can use me as you wish. I felt her energy join mine and she held Mikes toes, the immense feeling of love that swelled up inside of me, for Mike from his mother was phenomenal. I sent this love from my heart into Mikes and I knew he would feel this surge of love. I then continued working on Mike and worked back up towards his head.

When I was working on Mike's sacral chakra he opened his eyes for a second and looked at me. It was an intense healing session and if the energy was high starting off it was now palpable. When the session was complete I asked Mike how that had felt for him. He said it was amazing and so very relaxing. He told me that he had seen his mother standing at the end of the bed, with her hands on his feet. He spoke of the love he felt fill his heart in that moment and he welled up with emotion as the thought of this. Mike and his mom have a very special bond that death did not diminish. It was such an emotional, joyous, miraculous healing for Mike. I felt so blessed and grateful to have been a part of this wonderful magical experience. Mike went for a nap afterwards and I went out to the garden to sit in gratitude and do a little meditating. I took some photos of the birds, the sky and nature in general, before I came back indoors to begin cooking dinner. Later that evening I had my first international video call of medium ship to New York. I was a little nervous of how spirit would connect, when my client was so many miles away. It was an absolutely beautiful session; the conversation was just as if we were sitting in the same room. I need not have worried at all. Technology is awesome! Caroline is a beautiful Irish lady living in America and originally lived in County Kerry! The world really is a small place. Her dad came through for her with beautiful reassuring wisdom. He was a lovely and gentle man and there was great love between him and Caroline. What an amazing experience that was. Before going to bed I looked at the photos I had taken earlier and I was gob smacked by what I saw. There were the most spectacular rainbow clouds with angel and fairy orbs in each of the photos! It was absolutely breathtaking.

Today was filled with such blessings and so many of them I floated off to bed in a state of bliss. I woke before the alarm, full of the joys of life. I had faith that God was working everything out for us and that Mike would be ok. It was a glorious warm morning, the sky was blue without a cloud in the sky, the birds were singing their morning chorus and I sat giving thanks to God for the all these wonderful blessings he has given to me. I sat by a tree with my eyes closed and my heart was soaring out of my body, as I expressed deep gratitude for the blessing my life is. I had a busy day with clients for healings and readings. I felt so blessed to have met some wonderful new people and to have shared some very special moments with them. The rest of the month floated by in a blur of helping Mike to heal, shop work, the children, my clients and meditations, I look back now and I wonder how did I do all that, how did I manage to keep it all together, how did I manage to remain in faith and positive every single day? I thank God and the angels for without them I could have done none of it.

Friday July1ˢᵗ I held my second public medium ship demonstration in the same hotel as the first one. I had not set a limit on tickets this time as capacity was only a hundred I felt I could cope with that and anyway what was meant to be would be. Seventy three people attended on the night, it was amazing. The room was much bigger and brighter that the room on the first night, so I was thrilled with that. Spirit connections were strong and clear.

The night flowed fluidly and smoothly. Everyone enjoyed themselves and some very powerful healing messages came through. Everyone in the audience was lovely, as were their loved ones in spirit, it really was a magical night. The feedback was incredible, I was crowded by people thanking me and verifying information that had come through me from their loved ones in spirit. Everyone was happy for everyone else. Those who received messages were delighted and even those that had not, had such empathy for those that had, they felt happy for them. I felt so humbled at this outpouring of gratitude. My heart swelled with thanks, to all these wonderful people and their loved ones in spirit, for accepting me as I am. Life is truly magnificent!

The next morning I woke up feeling totally exhausted. I had three clients for medium ship sittings and that took all the strength I had in me. Thankfully they each were lovely people and I was so grateful for such beautiful healing experiences, encountered in my little angel room in the shop. I made a mental note to myself not to work on a day after a public demonstration of medium ship in platform style again. I needed to boost up my energy and take some nurturing time for me. Luckily the next day was Sunday and I planned to rest! I got out of bed at 8.30am and sat in meditation for half an hour. I then went outside to do my gratitude and, then fed the birds and the animals. I then lay on the couch reading a new Dr. Wayne Dyer book I had started a few days ago. The book was called *Change Your Thoughts, Change your Life*, I happily read for a few hours, relaxed and contented.

We had a late vegetarian breakfast of eggs, beans, hash browns and toast and decided we would drive to the beach and go for a walk there. We all piled into the car and drove for about an hour before landing at the beach. It was a glorious day; the sun was high in the sky and so warm. Not a cloud to be seen as far as the eyes could see. We walked for a few miles along the beach, laughing and talking, tickling and playing. We all soaked up the energy of the sea and felt much more energized. We stopped near a sand dune and the children started climbing with shrills of delight! Mike and I sat facing the Atlantic Ocean, the children were playing in the sand just off to my left.

The ocean was mesmerizing, just sitting and watching the waves was so peaceful and soothing to my soul. We walked to the waters edge and wet our feet for awhile. We were having so much fun together. Afterwards we went back and sat down it was time to eat. We had a little picnic of some fruit, a salad roll and some juice to wash it all down. Mike then went making sandcastles with the children. The craic' was mighty, as they collected shells and feathers for the sand castles they were creating. I took advantage of this time to meditate and spend some time with God. I sat up straight and crossed my legs as in a yoga pose, hands open on my lap, and eyes shut. It was blissful, relaxing to the sound of the waves and feeling the warmth of the sun and the light sea breeze on my skin was heavenly. I must have sat like this for the best part of an hour before the three amigos came back and brought me back to the land of the living! I felt so connected, loved and blessed. We chatted for a little while before gathering our things and walked back to the car. We stopped off at the local shop for an ice cream and we were all as contented as could be for the journey home. We were all feeling grateful for such a perfect day; it was like heaven on earth!

CHAPTER 8

Saint Pio

The next morning was Monday July 4th, I woke up before my alarm and sat in meditation for twenty minutes, and I then got dressed and ready for the day and went outside to give thanks for the beautiful new day. My heart was overflowing with gratitude for the many blessings my days were filled with. I had a full day in the shop today and there was a big delivery of angel products in, so that kept me busy pricing and merchandising all the new beautiful stock lines. Of course I purchased a few of those beauties for myself before I closed up the shop! I thought just a few more new angels, for one of my special places. I often think I am my own best customer!

After dinner I had a client for a healing. Bernadette was pregnant and was experiencing some pains. She was afraid and anxious about a premature delivery. I spoke to her and calmed her down and reassured her that everything would happen as it should and there was no need to worry. She said "I hope your right Jane!" as she hopped up on the therapy bed. As I stood at the head of the bed I prepared myself to begin the healing session. I said a prayer and called upon the Archangels Michael and Raphael to protect and heal her. Through closed eyes the room instantly filled with colours, beautiful vibrant purples, pinks and green. It was spectacular and the feeling of love and peace in the room was so powerful. It was absolutely breathtaking.

When I asked Bernadette afterwards how that felt for her? She replied" that was amazing. I have no pain now, it's incredible, and how did you do that? I can't describe how peaceful and calm I feel. If this baby decides to enter the world right now it would not bother me!" I laughed and said well that's a big turn around from when you arrived here!" She then said "can I say something; you might think I'm mad but I have to say this." I assured Bernadette that anything she said to me was in total confidentiality and I was not going to judge her in any way." She began to say, at first I had my eyes closed and saw the brightest purple, pink and green swirling around in front of my eyes, so I opened my eyes incase I was imagining it and I saw all those fabulous colours floating above me and I have felt this serene calmness since!" I replied "you are not going mad I saw the colours too, they were awesome! They are the colors of the Archangels and they were all helping to heal you." Bernadette said "Oh my God I knew it, I don't know how I knew it but I knew they were angels by the way I felt." We chatted some more and I wished her the best of everything and to contact me anytime if her worries returned.(Her baby Joseph was born on his due date two months later, perfect in every way.)

Afterwards I went in home and spent a little time with the children before they went to bed. I read them a story once they were tucked up tightly and said goodnight and came down stairs to the sitting room. I had a cup of tea with Mike before he went to work for the night. Once alone I decided to light some incense and a few candles and sit in meditation. I wanted to clear my mind and relax my body before going to bed. I cherish these moments in each day where I feel closer to God.

I went to bed at 10.30pm and fell asleep instantly. I awoke some hours later; I could sense someone else in the bedroom with me. I knew Mike was at work and it did not feel like one of my children. It felt more like the presence of spirit. I sleep on the right side of the bed, so I turned my head to look to my left to see who was there. I did not feel afraid or alarmed in any way.

What I saw was Padre Pio standing half way down the side of the bed. He was tall and broad, much bigger than I would have thought of him to be. He had one hand at his chest and his other hand held out as if towards me. He smiled at me, then blessed himself and extended his hand from that blessing out to me in blessing. In my head I said thank you Padre Pio, I am both honored and blessed in this moment, I blinked and he was gone! My heart was filled with so much love and peace; bliss is the nearest word that may describe how I felt. I looked at the clock to see what time it was, the clock read 4.44am .I said to myself I must check what that means in angel numbers in the morning and smiling went straight back to sleep.

I woke when the alarm went off and my mind instantly went back to Padre Pio standing in the room with me. Why had he visited me? Why had he blessed me? All the questions in my head, it was filled with them. I got up and thought I won't mediate today; my head is just too full of excitement and questions. So with a thought like that, I knew today of all days I needed to meditate so I sat for a long deep meditation. I went deep into meditation very quickly; I sat there for about forty minutes in blissful silence. This was absolutely amazing, I had never meditated so deep before, I could not wait to meditate again that night to experience it again.

When I saw Mike at lunch time I told him of Padre Pio's visit. Mike said "that's amazing sweetheart, you are blessed and so very lucky!" I agreed with Mike and I felt so humbled by it all. "Why do you think he came to bless me"? I asked Mike. He answered "I'm sorry I can't help you, I don't know, it's a miracle sweetheart!" I agreed that it was, it sure was a miracle! I had a client for healing after lunch so I drove home to an teach to do the healing and Mike worked the shop for me.

My client was referred to me by a friend of hers who had come to me. Julia began to cry as she tried to tell me why she needed to be here. She apologized and cried and cried some more. I sat quietly and let her get it all out; she would feel so much better after letting all of it out. She eventually stopped crying and went and lay into the bed. I covered her with a warmed blanket, and then took my position at the head of the bed. As soon as I put my hands on her head I got the most intense pain in my stomach, it nearly floored me! I took in a few deep breaths to help absorb the pain so I could focus on my client and the healing process taking place. The pain left after about ten minutes and I was able to carry on. She experienced a lovely movement of energy and a huge release of emotional and physical pain. When we spoke afterwards she told me she had suffered for months with ovarian cysts and with the excruciating pain from them. She was scheduled for an operation in two weeks time, unless the pain went before then. Her pain was now gone! "That's awesome" I said," no need for surgery now!" Julia rang me the next day and told me she was over the moon to be pain free and able to bend down and do normal things again, you are a miracle worker Jane! I met Julia a few months later and she told me that she never needed the surgery after all and never had any pain again either!

After Julia's healing that afternoon I was busy cleaning the house. I was teaching my first class of reiki 1 students at home the next day. I pretty much forgot about Padre Pio, as I scrambled to get everything in place and ready for my six students. Cleaning and polishing until bedtime. The next morning I woke before the alarm and felt so excited. Today was the day I would teach reiki to six wonderful ladies. I was not a bit nervous, just excited! I had the History of Reiki booklets printed out for them and their reiki 1 manual. The fridge was packed with food for lunch with every concoction of salad and some nice cakes.

Everyone arrived one after the other and all within a few moments of each other. Each of the ladies was an amazing, caring, beautiful and sensitive woman. The day just flew by, we had so much fun and some awesome healings occurred. The excitement of this new beginning for all the students was a strong for me as it was for each of them individually. I knew the magic that awaited them. After they all left I tidied up a little then sat in meditation to give thanks for this beautiful, blessed and special day. I then prayed for all the newly attuned healers that their wishes would materialize for themselves and their families. As crazy as this may sound, I did not think about Padre Pio's visit again until the Saturday night after!

Mike rang me from work and asked me if I would like to go to the healing well in north Kerry the next day. I said "Oh yes, that is a great idea,I'd love to go because I want to go to the church and talk to Padre Pio's statue and see can I get some answers as to why he appeared to me ".We agreed that, that was what we would do. The next day we set off for the healing well and as per every time we have ever been there, the sun came out and it was a beautiful day. I took out my phone to take a few pictures of the beautiful well and the Archangel Michael.

I pressed the camera icon on my phone to open the app and instead of opening the camera it took a photograph. That's very strange I thought so I pressed it again and the same thing happened! What was going on? How was this even possible I thought? Third time lucky I pressed it again and this time the camera opened like it always should. When I looked at those first two photos the phone took itself, they were filled with orbs so I knew it all had to do with the angels! I sat for a while, and at first I had my eyes closed and saw the brightest purple, pink and green swirling around in front of my eyes. This was so beautiful. After some time we walked back to the car and drove a little further on to the church.

Inside the church was a Padre Pio room with a life size statue of Saint Pio and that was what I had come to see. It was a beautiful room with very ornate stained glass windows. The sun was shining through the stained glass and the room looked full with colors. There were four chairs in front of the window facing the statue and to the side of them was a stand with candles for intentions. Next to that was a first class relic in a glass case of the heart bandage of Padre Pio. The statue itself is standing on a water pedestal with constant flowing water, with a kneeler in front of it and at either side of the statue is some writing on Saint Pio and some lovely prayers. It truly is a beautiful room and the energy felt so peaceful and healing, it was so beautiful. The four of us entered the room together and took a seat in front of the window facing the statue of Saint Pio. We sat in silence for a little while, each with our own private thoughts and reflections. That became too much for the young ones, who were getting itchy feet and noisy mouths. Mike said he would take Hannah and Michael for a walk outside, to give me sometime on my own with Saint Pio. I began by saying some prayers and then I looked at the statue and began to talk with Saint Pio. Silently and with pure intention of heart I said "Thank you so very much Saint Pio for appearing to me. I feel very grateful to you for your presence and the generous blessing you gave to me. I don't know what I should do about it though; I do feel you want me to share this story to help others with their faith, and to heal them. If this is so what should I do? I am going to take some photographs, Saint Pio will you show me something in the next photograph I take, if you want me to do something more since your visit to me or something different than I am already doing. Thank you." I took my phone out of my handbag and went into the camera on it. I took one photograph and then another. I then put my phone back in my handbag and read the prayers on the wall. I then sat in quiet meditation for a little while. The feeling of love and peace that I felt at that time was phenomenal and time seemed to have stopped.

Twenty minutes later Michael came running in to the room and asked me if I was finished. I told him I was almost finished, I would be ready in one minute. I then stood and silently said to Saint Pio as I looked into the statues eyes, "Thank you Saint Pio for this wonderful experience and for the gift of your blessing." I then took Michael by the hand and we walked out of the room and out of the church. We were half way home when I thought again of the photograph. The one I had asked Saint Pio to give me a sign in it. I took my phone out of my handbag and went in to gallery to see the photograph. I scrolled to the photograph and I almost dropped my phone.

My heart was in my mouth, as it almost jumped out of my chest. "Oh my God," is all I managed to say out loud. I could hardly breathe. Saint Pio was alive! I was looking at him in the flesh not a statue! I said to Mike "he has hair" and Mike replied "Who are you talking about"? I said "Saint Pio's beard is hair, actual hair –not plastic. Mike put on his indicator and pulled the car onto the side of the road. I handed my phone to Mike and he looked at the photograph and said "This is a miracle, Oh my God!" We zoomed in and out of the photograph noticing different details. This was absolutely incredible. I had half expected to see an orb or angel light in the photograph, nothing in my wildest of dreams prepared me for a real life Saint Pio to be looking back at me! After a while Mike restarted the car and continued on the journey home. I could not stop smiling, this was such a miracle! I closed my eyes and tried to calm myself, I was still finding it hard to breathe. I silently thanked Saint Pio, for this most beautiful and treasured gift and blessing. He had given me a clear answer that I was to share my story of his visit, his blessing and now his miracle! There are no words to describe how blessed I feel at this occurrence and events. My mind was blown away by Saint Pio's miracle.

That night after the little ones had gone to bed, I turned on the computer to read up on Saint Pio. I really did not know much about him at all. I listened to a Padre Pio prayer and meditation and then went to bed myself. I was exhausted after the huge excitement of the day. I did not sleep well at all that night. There was a lot of spirit activity just outside my bedroom door and in the room later on all around me. I could not see any spirit in the room but I could feel them and hear them. I crawled out of bed the next morning, I was so tired. I went outside to soak up some energy from nature and to give thanks for my many blessings, which were now growing by the day! It was a beautiful morning, with clear blue sky and the sun was shining. The birds were singing beautiful melodies and all was well in my world, as I sat here in quiet reflection. I then went inside and sat in meditation. I went deep very quickly and for along time. It was the most intense and deep meditation I had ever experienced, I was completely zoned out for half an hour. I then had to get ready for the shop so normality was back with a bang. I did all the chores that needed to be done in the shop and then some light dusting. I made myself a cup of lemon and ginger tea and went online to see if I could find out who the parish priest was over that church with the Saint Pio's room.

I felt that I should tell him of the miracle that occurred in his church yesterday. I found his details and wrote down his name and phone number. I held off ringing him, I thought I should ask Mike first, when I saw him what he thought I should do regarding talking to the priest. Mike is my rock and a lot more sensible than me sometimes so I trust his opinion. Later after lunch I said it to Mike that I was going to ring the priest and tell him about the miracle. Mike thought I should keep it to myself, that it was not information to be shared. He felt that for my own protection I should not ring the priest, he felt the priest would probably not even believe me. I should keep it to myself for now. I knew as Mike spoke that I just had to ring the priest, in my heart and soul I knew this was what I was meant to do. I said to Mike, "I don't care if he does not believe me; this is not about me or even about the priest, it's all about Saint Pio and the miracle that took place in the church."

Once I decided I was definitely going to ring the parish priest I felt sick with nerves. What if he didn't believe me or if he thought I was crazy? I put all these questions out of my head as

I keyed in the priests phone number. It rang and rang; I think I might have stopped breathing as I waited for him to answer his mobile! Then he answered and said" hello", I introduced myself to him and told him I was in his lovely Saint Pio room in his lovely church yesterday. I told him an event had happened there that I wished to tell him about. He said "ok you can tell me." I said "I have to go back to something that brought me to the church yesterday so you get the full story so please bear with me. On the early hours of Tuesday July 5th Padre Pio appeared to me as I lay in my bed. I had gone to bed at 10.30pm and I had woken hours later knowing there was a spirit presence in the room. When I looked to my left Padre Pio was standing there. He smiled at me blessed himself then extended his had towards me in blessing". Father then said "I'm very sorry but I did not hear all of that" so I repeated it word for word again. There was then the longest silence as I waited for the priest to reply. I took the phone from my ear to check if the call was still connected, it was so I just waited and waited silently for another minute or so. It was the longest few minutes of my life and my nerves were not helping! When he spoke he said " I'm sorry for the quietness there, I am in someone's house on a house call and I could not answer you, but I have your number and I will ring you back later on .Thank you for calling me and God Bless". I replied "Thank you father I'll speak with you again then".

I waited all evening for him to ring back. My phone coverage at home was very poor so I thought he may not have been able to get through so by 8pm I gave up on the idea he was going to ring. I decided I would ring him again the next day to finish what I had begun to tell him. At 9 pm I went outside to get some phone coverage, I wanted to ring my friend Pamela. A few years ago she had leant me a book and that was the first I ever had read regarding Padre Pio. Her father had a great devotion to St Pio. She told me around that time she would lend me a book, she felt I would enjoy. So one day in early 2014 she came into the shop, and handed me a brown paper bag with the book inside of it. I said "thank you, oh what's that beautiful smell?" she said "what does it smell like?" and I replied "it's like flowers or roses, its beautiful is it your perfume?" She laughed and said "are you kidding me?" I said "no why?" She said" the name of the book is about the scent of Roses", and that is what people smell when Padre Pio is near". The smell was gone now so I replied" maybe it's not that then".

I had not thought of or remembered this conversation until that night that I was outside going to tell her of the visit and the church. I did not remember anything much from the book either; it was as if I never read it! I rang Pamela and she answered almost straight away. We had not seen each other for ages and hadn't had much chats in between either, so we did a little bit of general chit chat first. Then I told her of all that happened with me and Saint Pio. She was totally amazed, almost speechless! She had been praying to Saint Pio all day and asked him for a sign, and now here I was telling her this." This is my sign" she said. She was absolutely shocked and delighted to receive this news after waiting all day for a sign. We tried to figure it all out, to no avail and I told her I would let her know what the priest would say to me tomorrow.

My phone received a voicemail just then at ten o clock. I clicked to listen to the voicemail which had been left at seven thirty pm. It was from the priest. I listened to the recording, he said" Thank you Jane for speaking with me this morning and that was a truly wonderful experience for you. There is no need to ring me back .Goodbye and God Bless". What a time to have no network coverage I thought, but as everything happens for a reason I would stick to my earlier plan and ring him again tomorrow. I went inside and sat in meditation for half an hour, again I went very deep. It was an amazingly beautiful experience.

The next day was Tuesday and I woke before the alarm. I got up early and sat in quiet meditation; I loved these deeper meditations and could not wait to do each one. I felt so connected to my guides, my guardian angel, the angels, the archangels, the Saints and God. I knelt for my prayers that morning and it was almost meditative, it was an intensely spiritual experience. After eleven am I rang the priest again. I introduced myself again and he said he had left me a voice mail did I receive it I said "Thank you father I did receive your voicemail" he said "oh that's good so there was no need to ring me again." I replied "but I had not finished my story so I needed to ring you back". He said "you told me of Padre Pio visiting you so can carry on from there". I proceeded to tell him of what had happened in the church on Sunday and the statue coming to life .I also told him I had a photograph of this occurrence. He asked me a few questions and we talked for a little while. He then agreed to meet with me two Sundays from then, on July 24th, so he could see the photograph himself. I was kept busy all the rest of the week with the shop and clients.

Thursday July14th was the second class of reiki 1. I was teaching and this time I had some male and some female students. It was a beautiful day and everyone was lovely. It was amazing to hear all the different stories that brought each one to me on that day. They could not have been more different! I was giving the reiki 1 attunement to one lady called Vivian when I was guided to keep my hands on her shoulder for longer than required. I stayed with it for as long as I felt was needed then carried on with her attunement. After her attunement she was thrilled.

She had such a beautiful spiritual experience during her attunement as she was very sensitive to energy. She said" you have cured my shoulder" as she maneuvered and manipulated her right shoulder. She said "I have had that pain for months and months and you hardly touched me and now it's gone, wow lady you are so good!" I was very happy for Vivienne. She told all the others of the agony she had suffered with her shoulder injury for so long and that it was now healed, she was amazed! The day was full of meditating, healings, teaching and learning. I was much more relaxed and confident as a teacher for the second time. It's amazing how quickly we can get used to things, when we get over our fears. I felt so very grateful after everybody went home, so I sat in meditation for a while. I love what I now do, I love helping people, I love all the awesome amazing healers I meet and teach. I love working from home, having more time with my family, my life felt so blessed. I remembered reading it somewhere that once you invite the angels into your life, your life becomes a blessing. Oh my, yes my life had indeed become a blessing in every sense of the word. I spent the rest of the evening having fun with the children. Hannah helped me to cook the dinner and Michael helped me set the table, while Mike set up the fire, such a perfect day! Mike and I did a guided meditation before he went to work. I then went to bed with my heart and soul full of love and gratitude.

The next morning I woke before the alarm, full of the joys of life! This seemed to be becoming a habit and I loved it. It was not all that long ago, a few short years ago that I had to crawl out of bed as late as possible, usually the last minute and drag myself off to work. That afternoon I had a client from Sweden. Louise was in agony with her back. She was unable to lie down so I propped her with pillows to have her as comfortable as possible.

As soon as I placed my hands on her head I felt nauseous, I intuited that this was from the severity of the pain she was in. I have no idea how exactly I knew this, but I knew that I knew it! After a few minutes her pain came through me, it began in my lower back and travelled the whole way down my right leg to my toes. It was excruciating, I felt unsure if I could stay standing. I asked the angels for extra assistance and called on Archangel Michael to give me enough strength to carry out this healing as Louise was in agony. I carried on with the healing and for the best part of the hour the pain was present, when I felt her pain go I finished the healing session. Louise said she felt absolutely amazing. She said she had never felt so relaxed in her entire life. She had even managed to doze off to sleep for part of the healing and said her sleep was so peaceful. When she sat up her mobility seemed better, and then she swung her legs to the side of the bed. This amazed her as she had been unable to do that for months! I advised her to take it easy for a few days as I sensed she may tend to overdo it with her new reclaimed mobility.

A few days later she came in to the shop to me and started twirling around and jumping up and down. Smiling from ear to ear she said "Jane I don't know what you did to me but look at me!" The change was remarkable; I did not recognize her as the same Louise I had met for the first time a few days ago. It came to me later that evening that my healings and meditations and prayers all had deepened in the past few weeks, I wondered had it anything to do with Saint Pio and the blessing he had given me? Mike and I began to discuss building a bigger healing room in the shop. My little angel reading room was too small for a therapy bed. That meant I was driving home eight miles for healings and then back to the shop afterwards. It also meant Mike driving from home to cover the shop and then leaving the shop to go home when I came back in! I was getting new clients everyday now and I was very busy with healings. It made sense not to be doing all that driving. Also traffic was so busy and then some clients got lost so a lot of time was being wasted.

We picked a corner of the shop where the new healing room would go and made a strategy for selling down sections to allow room for this healing room. Mike drew up some plans and priced the job, he would create the room himself so it was just building supplies he priced. I am so grateful for Mike; he can turn his hand to anything. I felt so excited at this new expansion of my healings. Jane's Healing Room would be ready for business within the month in Donnelly's Shop Killarney!

I held another Meet your Guardian Angel Workshop. There were six students booked in for that day. It was myself and all the other earth angels for the day. These beautiful ladies had amazing auras of healing and light. The energy in the room was incredible for the entire day. The angels definitely made their presence known to us. I treated all the ladies to a fifteen minute angel healing each after lunch. They were all amazed at how good they felt after this little time of healing. Whilst healing the ladies I felt as if I was up there with the angels and the sensations were incredible. The room was filled with purple and green from the Archangels Michael and Raphael. The most vibrant of colours! It was fantastic to see! All of these ladies are blessings to everyone they meet. We had an awesome day together and with the angels.

That night as I sat in meditation I felt so grateful for the day I had and for the deepening in all my spiritual gifts. This just had to be from Saint Pio I thought and the blessing I felt in that moment I knew it to be true. My heart was overflowing with gratitude to Saint Pio and to God, I don't know why this happened to me or why, but I was deeply humbled by the entire experience. The next day I had three clients, all booked in for healings. Christina my last client of the day arrived at eight pm. This was her second visit to me and I really did not recognize her straight away, she looked so different! She visibly looked at least ten years younger. She even looked taller! She said she had been feeling fantastic since she had come to me, until yesterday so she needed a pick me up today. As I placed my hands on her head I saw the brightest white light at times then it transformed into a pyramid shape of blue and purple lights, I was loosing awareness as I worked on her, getting drawn very deep into the healing. The hour went by very fast; it seemed to me to be about twenty minutes maximum had passed, so I was very surprised when I saw the time. When I finished up and asked Christina how she felt now? She answered "Oh my God Jane what did you do? It is the most incredible feeling I have ever had. Those lights of white, blue and purple felt so warm and healing. Did I imagine them?"

I assured Christina that it was not her imagination, that I too had experienced that beautiful feeling and seen the colors too. I spoke to her of my experience with Saint Pio and I said that I felt the intensity of today's session must have something to do with that. She was amazed by my story and she told me that she herself prayed to Padre Pio every day. Afterwards I thanked Saint Pio and God for such an awesome healing for her, she so deserved it. Life had been very trying for her up to now. The next day I had a full day of medium ship sittings. Word of mouth was getting out there strongly now, regarding my healings and medium ship skills. Each of my clients was a lovely and genuine person. Their readings were deeply personal and moving. Their loved ones in spirit were salt of the earth types of people and their messages were full of so much love. It was an amazing day and so much healing had taken place, so much faith revived, so much comfort given, so many prayers answered and so much more occurred. I felt as though my heart could take no more blessings, it was full. I was so humbled and honored to be the voice of spirit for such beautiful people.

The next day was Sunday, the day I had arranged to meet with the parish priest of the church. I woke up at seven am and spent a long time in prayer and meditation. I was feeling excited and nervous at the same time. What if he was not a nice person? Or if he said he could not see what everyone who had seen the picture saw? I stopped this negative thinking and put full trust in God and Saint Pio that they had guided me to this day. It would be grand! I went outside and fed the birds and the hens, then sat by a tree in solitude. It was a beautiful day and I took in all the beauty of nature all around. Nature is so healing, I felt it salve my soul and settle me down. It was heavenly just sitting there blending in with nature. Before I knew it, it was time to get in the car and go meet the priest. I was feeling calm and confident as Mike drove us there.

Mass was still on when we arrived at the church so Mike parked up and we waited in the car, for everyone to leave the church when mass ended. When we thought everyone must be out we walked in to the church. A few people were chatting inside so we took a seat at the back of the church. When everyone had left, I saw a nice man at the top of the church clearing things away. I said to Mike "Will I ask him where the priest is?" Mike said "yes, go up to him, do what you came here to do and we will wait here for you, best of luck sweetheart". I left Mike with Hannah and Michael and walked up to the man and I told him I was here to see the priest and that I had an appointment. He showed me into a room off the side of the church and told me he was in there, just walk in to him. The door was opened but I knocked anyway, the priest turned around and shook my hand as we introduced ourselves. He brought me to a room further back from the church and offered me a seat while he went to get another seat for himself. I reminded him of our conversation of Saint Pio's visit to me and the statue coming alive. I told him I printed out the photographs and as I handed them to him I explained one was of the statue as it is now and the other is of Saint Pio, when I asked for a sign from him.

He looked at both photographs then focused on the real life one. His eyes teared up and after a long moment he looked at me and said" This is spectacular "and I nodded in agreement. After a while he said "Did you take these photographs with an ordinary camera?" Pointing at the photographs in his hands I nervously said "I took those photos with my phone". "Dear God" he said "this is amazing" I said "it is a miracle" and he then said "Yes it is, it is indeed a miracle! He then looked at the photo for another few minutes then he turned to me and said "Padre Pio has chosen you to be a proponent of his in this time. By showing himself to you, this is what he meant. You have very special gifts that God has given you. God has chosen you to do his work and Padre Pio will guide you. He will help you to do this. I told him of the day, I received the holy water from the well and the day; I had a vision of his church whilst Mike was driving to the healing well. He then asked me to tell him a bit more about myself. So I told him I was married to Mike and have four children, I run my own shop that sells angels,crystals, holy pictures and all things spiritual and angelic, I am a healer and I do energy healings and I am medium, I can communicate with spirit and the angels.

He said "You are clearly a remarkable lady, protect your energy and be mindful of unsavory people. You have so many special gifts, and many ways to do God's work. I do not have any of these gifts even though my life is dedicated to God. And my life's mission is to do Gods work. You are capable of doing great works for God". I said "thank you so much for your kind and lovely words". He then asked me if it would be ok with me if placed his hands on my head and gave me a blessing. I told him I would gratefully accept his blessing. He then stood up and walked behind my chair. He placed his two hands on the top of my head. The energy that surged through my crown chakra, right through my body was incredible. I closed my eyes and openly received this generous blessing. He began to pray in Latin, and then I saw Padre Pio in my minds eye and felt a pressure on my nose and under my eyes. It felt like a new spirit guide, only covering a larger area. I relaxed and absorbed this blessing which I'm not sure how long it lasted as I was deeply relaxed. The priest then spoke to me again and said" it is not for us to ask God why? And God never picks rich or seemingly overly important people to do his work. When we look at Lourdes or Fatima we can see evidence of this. Even Saint Pio himself was not from riches. You have been chosen by God. May God bless you in the work you do and keep you safe". I said "Thank you very much father, I am very grateful that you could meet with me today".

We walked down to the Padre Pio Room and sat in prayer there. We were silent for a time, then the priest stood up and made a sign of the cross in the water, under Saint Pio's statue and walked to me and made a sign of the cross on my forehead .Then he said "May God bless you Jane and thank you for thinking of us here and sharing your photograph, we truly appreciate it." I replied "thank you father for all you have given me today, and may God bless you also". He smiled and with a small wave of his hand he left me there. My heart and mind was full from all he had said. I felt overwhelmed. I did not consider myself worthy of this blessing and such a gift from God. I looked at Saint Pio and I asked him to help me step into the best version of me, so I could do this work that both he and God felt I could do. Then I thought- no one probably ever does feel worthy, when they receive a blessing like this. I thanked him for choosing me to guide and support. I then promised him, that I would not let him down and together we would do as God has planned.

I went outside then to look for Mike and the children. I found them behind the church in the little graveyard for priests. I had not realized how long I had been in talking with the priest, so I apologized to Mike for being gone so long. Mike said they had all got on very well and kept themselves entertained, so it was all good. Mike then asked me "how did it go" and I answered him "awesome"! I did not want to talk about it in front of the little ones just yet, so we decided to drive to the beach where Mike and I could talk in private. When we got to the beach there was an ice cream shop there, so we got some ice cream cones for Hannah and Michael, they ran ahead laughing and screeching as the licked their ice creams. I then told Mike all that had happened in the church. Mike was amazed and delighted.

He was so pleasantly surprised at this open and caring man's attitude towards me and in such a kind and supportive way that he had treated me. He said that the priest was obviously a very true and holy man; I agreed that I was blessed to have met and received a blessing from such a gentle man of God. The children stopped at a sand dune and wanted to play there, so I helped them get their shoes and socks off. They ran up the sand and slid back down with whoops and hollers of glee. Mike and I sat just to the side of the sand dune, so we could see the little ones safely, as well as the ocean and the beach. It was a magnificent day and to be at the beach was such a special treat, it was so warm and the sun was splitting the stones. Not a cloud to be seen, just blue sky.

The water was so calm, ebbing and flowing onto the sand, so mesmerizing to watch. Mike and I discussed what it all could mean, what the priest had said to me was phenomenal! After a while I lay down and closed my eyes. The heat of the sun on my body was gorgeous. I relaxed and breathed in the clear salty air from the Atlantic Ocean. I could hear the waves from the sea, the children laughing and playing, birds singing and a dog barking in the distance. Everything was well in my world and I was feeling totally blessed. I meditated for a while then I silently began to talk to Saint Pio. I welcomed him to my life and thanked him for his presence in it. I felt him connect with me and I was filled with such intense feelings of peace and love. I was no longer aware of where I was, or even how long I was in this blissful state. When I came back to conscious awareness, I thanked God for sending Saint Pio to assist me with my life's purpose. I prayed for the inner strength and wisdom that I would need for this task. I then thanked both God and Saint Pio for their complete faith in me. I could sense the changes that would come my way in the very near future. Suddenly I knew my future was wide open!

Thanks Be to God

AFTERWORD

It was on the 4th[th] of January 2017, early in the morning when I sat in meditation that Saint Pio connected with me. He told me that I could help more people if I wrote a book .I thanked him for this guidance and seriously thought that yes, I would indeed begin to write of my experience with Saint Pio. He is loved and devoted by so many people all over the world. The following day Mike came in from clearing the garage and handed me a two hard back copies, he said you might have use for these. I laughed as I replied "thank you honey, I have plans for them already!" Mike looked at me surprised as he said "really sweetheart?" I then told him of my meditation time the morning before and Saint Pio's guidance to me. Mike thought it was a great idea and he said he would work in the shop a few days a week for me, so I could concentrate on writing the book. We both marveled at how Mike was guided to give me the copies! Life is funny! Michaels 6th birthday was the next day so all thoughts of the book left my head, we would celebrate after work with a little party and on Sunday take him wherever he wanted to go. I had four clients booked in for healings in Jane's Healing Room in the shop, so it was a full day ahead. The first client Mary was suffering bereavement and was in a lot of deep emotional pain. Saint Pio appeared as soon as I placed my hands on her head. Her healing was very powerful. I asked her after if she prayed to Saint Pio, she replied, that she always carried his prayer card with her and said that prayer daily. When I told her Saint Pio was in the room at the beginning of

111

her healings she was delighted. The next client another Mary was feeling stuck in her life; nothing seemed to be working out recently for her. As soon as I laid my hands on her head Saint Pio appeared, he showed me her holding a rosary and praying. Her healing session was very intense and there was a lot of heat released. Afterwards I asked her if she prayed to Saint Pio, she said yes and I then told her what Pio had shown me. She was amazed and delighted to know Saint Pio heard her prayers. My next client was Bernie from Dublin. I had first met Bernie on Christmas Eve at 5pm, when her husband David brought her to me for a healing. Bernie was a retired teacher and had in the past year suffered a stroke and it had affected her confidence hugely.

That day as Bernie was wheeled in to the shop in her wheelchair, I really did not recognize this glamorous bright eyed lady as Bernie, she looked amazing and nothing like how frightened and listless she had been two weeks before! David was saying how happy they both were with Bernie's progress, since she had seen me two weeks ago. Both physically and in herself, she was feeling much happier. David helped Bernie onto the bed from her wheelchair and then he left us to begin the session. Again as soon as I put my hands on Bernie's head, Saint Pio appeared. He showed me her praying and said to tell her to continue with her prayers. Bernie was able to become very relaxed and had a very good healing session. Afterwards I said to her of Saint Pio and what he told me to tell her. This made sense to Bernie and she was overwhelmed with joy, that her prayers were answered. With a little help from me, she was able to take a few steps back to her wheelchair and sit down. It really was quiet remarkable to see these visible improvements in her. Last time she could hardly move! When David returned he was very surprised to see Bernie back in her chair. He was even more surprised to hear that Bernie had done it mostly by herself. When they had left, Mike handed me a piece of paper with a phone number on it.

A lady called Melody from Waterford wanted to see meet me, she had overheard Bernie and David when they first came through the shop and was very impressed with the improvements in Bernie she heard about. I rang Melody and she said she would come to me in ten minutes, she was unsure what she wanted, a reading or a healing. I cleaned down the room and then freshened it up, while I waited for her to arrive. Almost all my clients were with Saint Pio today I thought, that must mean something special, and what a day with Saint Pio appearing for clients it was so far! They were all so blessed.

Melody arrived and we shook hands and then sat in the healing room. Melody began to tell me how she found me today, was by pure accident. It was her husband that guided her into my shop, but once Melody heard about me she just had to see me and she did not know why. I suggested maybe some Angel cards for guidance, as she really did not know why she was with me and I did not feel a medium ship would benefit her that day. She told me a little about herself, she is a lovely, genuine lady. She told me then that her sister passed away some time ago and that she had always loved Padre Pio, and since her passing Melody was getting great comfort from churches and from Padre Pio. I then said to Melody" I know why you are here; it's because of Padre Pio." I then went on to tell Melody of the night Saint Pio visited me, about the day in the church, when the statue came to life and then the day I met the priest. She cried and cried. She then said that was all she needed to hear from me, she found such healing in hearing of these miracles. I told her a little about myself and she suggested a book on Padre Pio that she felt I would love to read. She felt I might find similarities with myself and Saint Pio's early life. I then connected to the angels for Melody and she received beautiful messages from them to help her in her grief and other areas of her life. Before leaving Melody said to me" you should advertise your story with Saint Pio or put a poster outside your shop or online to let people know. It would heal a lot of people, just as it has done for me she said." I knew this was a sign for me to write the book and I thanked her for her suggestions. We never meet people by chance; I knew Melody was guided to me to say those words. I was definitely going to buy that book on Padre Pio's life she had recommended. It was after 6.30pm when I left the shop that day. What an amazing day it had been! Everything was about Saint Pio and his miracles today. I felt so blessed to be able to help all these people and humbled that Saint Pio works through me, when he needs to connect with people's souls to help them heal. So many blessed clients today, it was phenomenal.

I felt exhausted once I sat down after dinner and went off to bed early that night. The following Friday I received an email from Balboa Press. I knew that I was meant to go with this as soon as I opened the email. I felt it in my soul. I showed Mike the email, when he came in the shop later in the day and he said "ring the number and see what the story is." I said "I'll ring it on Monday". Mike went off to the school to collect Hannah and Michael, and I thought about the publishing deal, I decided there and then to dial the number and keyed in the extension for Roberts office. The phone rang then went into voicemail so I left a message "Hello Robert, I'm Jane Donnelly and I live in Ireland. I received an email from you and I am very interested to hear more on a publishing contract. I do not have my book written yet, but I have started it. Thank you". I was so excited; I just knew this was going to be. On Monday afternoon January 16th, Robert returned my call and I told him a little about me and what my book was about, he then told me about Balboa Press and explained a lot of publishing details to me and by the time we finished talking that day, I had signed the contract with Balboa Press for a publishing deal on this book "Saint Pio's Blessing".

BIOGRAPHY

Jane Donnelly DIP/Psych holds Diplomas in Psychology, Counselling and Therapy, Angel Therapy and Crystal Healing, Aromatherapy and Sound Healing. Jane can see and communicate with both the Angels and with spirit. She is also a Reiki Master and Teacher. Jane is a Spirit Medium and has had this ability since childhood. She runs workshops, teaching students healing modalities, spiritual development and Meet your Guardian Angel day classes. Jane lives with her husband Mike and two of their children, Hannah and Michael. They live in County Kerry Ireland.

Printed in the United States
By Bookmasters